COMMUNICATIONS AND INFORMATION SECTORS, CASH-COWS TO THE NATION'S TREASURY

A **business-economic** and an **administrative perspective** to generate **wealth** and **employments** guide through **reforms**

A CASE STUDY OF NIGERIA

AMUSA

ABDULATEEF

Author of 'IF I ASPIRE TO LEAD' and 'RESTRUCTURING OF EDUCATION, ECONOMY, POLITICS, JUDICIARY AND RESOURCE CONTROL'

COPYRIGHT© 2015 AMUSA ABDULATEEF

Published by ADDIN RESOURCES VENTURES IBADAN, NIGERIA

080 5671 0944   080 3215 5018

addinrv@gmail.com latlib222@yahoo.com

Visit www.amusa-abdulateef.com for our books.

ISBN 9781979244879

All Rights Reserved. No part of this publication may be reproduced, distributed, or transmitted in any form or by any means, including photocopying, recording, or any other electronic or mechanical methods, without the prior written permission of the author.

TABLE OF CONTENTS

THE MISSION STATEMENT OF COMMUNICATIONS MINISTRY

PREFACE

CHANGE IS INEVITABLE

ACKNOWLEDGEMENT

DEDICATION

SYNOPSIS

PART ONE

WHAT IS COMMUNICATIONS AND INFORMATION TECHNOLOGY?

BENEFICIARIES OF THE COMUNICATIONS TECHNOLOGY

FUNCTIONS OF COMMUNICATIONS AND INFORMATION TECHNOLOGY TO NATIONAL DEVELOPMENTS

SOCIAL FUNCTIONS

ECONOMIC FUNCTIONS

POLITICAL AND ADMINISTRATIVE FUNCTIONS

PART TWO

COMMUNICATIONS AND INFORMATION MINISTRY: NIGERIA'S HISTORY

IDEALS OF THE MINISTRY

REGULATORY INSTITUTION UNDER THE MINISTRY

PART THREE

COMMUNICATIONS AND INFORMATION MINISTRY; A CASH COW?

PART FOUR

TROUBLESHOOTING, CAUSES AND SOLUTIONS IN REFORMS

THE FIVE-PRONGED REFORMS

PART FIVE

EXERCISE AND TESTS

AD-COPY AND REFERENCES

THE MISSION STATEMENT OF COMMUNICATIONS MINISTRY

The **mission statement** of the communication ministry is "to facilitate universal ubiquitous and cost effective access to communication infrastructures throughout the nation while promoting the utilization of ICT in all spheres of life to optimize the communications infrastructures."

These communication infrastructures as described above includes: digital content creation, domestic software applications the delivery of private and public services over the internet, promotion and facilitation of the development of the ICT industry increase in the contribution of the ICT industry to GDP, ICT to drive transparency in governance and improve the quality and cost effectiveness of public service delivery in Nigeria.

PREFACE

Developing and underdeveloped nations have common challenges in the funding of laudable projects. The problem has pushed them into debts with stringent conditions. Unfortunately, the corrupt malpractices from self-enrichment at the expense of the nation by the civil and public servants have become a big factor in the blockage of alternatives to borrowing as presented to the nation in form of proposal showing how the nation would be earning enough to fund the budget. The contents of this work were rejected by the people at the corridors of power simply because what we introduced would put an end to economic and finance crimes especially stealing and diversion of public funds. I could recall that the analytical findings of the research about the poor nations confirm that they can tap the knowledge-based economy by improving on taxation economy. As a result of my love for the nation, the proposals were sent to the right authorities at different ministries but unfortunately none was never acknowledged until I decided to publish this work in a book for every eyes to see and every mind to learn from. What do I mean? Those public and civil servant never allowed the message to fly because it would put an abrupt end to the sleaze money into their private accounts at the expense of the nation, Nigeria. This is their fear and this is my joy which is to eliminate individual and institutions that are richer when the nation is getting poorer by the day despite the opportunities to earn trillions from taxes and other revenues to the coffers of the nation useful to execute projects that would impact generations.

The book targets at introducing cashless economy especially in the deduction of all revenues from all the revenue base of the government through the use of apps. This could look like a hard task without adequate information about the data of the nationals and the institutions within. Another is the problem of tracking the sales and payments. But, are these impossible with the professional experts in the two ministry whose works the other ministries, departments and agencies must use for not less than 100% performance? There are things to put in place to achieve this. Such include the provision of working communication and information infrastructures, the right legislation and the power of autonomy for the revenue services to be independent without any internal and external influences. The book is worth research upon for the professional experts and institutes. This is a work that would serve as eyes opener for all nations borrowing to sustain the economies and other structures. The e-payment system should be embraced by the States or provincial governments, profit-based businesses and charity-based institutions too to eliminate financial crimes through diversion of money into private accounts at the peril of the institutions-**Author**

ACKNOWLEDGEMENT

All appreciations for the Almighty God for guiding me into the researches and provision of the strengths and supports to turn the works into book for the use of the nations. I acknowledge all my supporting pillars. To my inestimable jewel who always provide the safety net, Kudirah Joy Oladipupo; my children, Abdulaziz Ayomide and Sheriff Ayokunmi. I say thank you all for your enduring and supports.

I would never forget to acknowledge those who had positive impacts in my life from acquiring formal and religion education in the persons of late Mr. Abdulgafar Bello; Mrs. Kafilah Ibikunle and her husband, Mr. Kehinde Ibikunle; Mr. Bayo Olafusi; Mrs. Tomilayo Laniya, Proprietress of Bloom foundation group of schools; Mrs. Felicia Modupe Adeleke Proprietress of Nickdel group of schools; Mrs. Anike Abe and her ever lively family; Alhaji Iziaq Kunle Sanni and his dear spouse, Alhaja Rafat Idowu Kunle Sanni; Mr. Abdurazaq Busari-Olaoye, Alh. Bayo Azeez of procurement department of the ministry of health, Oyo State, Mr. Babatunde Alade (Dad Farouk) among others. They all played great roles, moral and financial in the becoming of a reputable writer and author.

Lest I forget to mention my good friends indeed as they are all around me at the time of need in the persons of Major Jimoh Oseni Folayemi ex-Chairman, NULGE of Odigbo Local Government, Ore; Mr. Olalekan Awujoola, Principal System Analyst Nigeria Defence Academy Kaduna State; Mr. Tiamiyu Abiodun of Nigeria International School Cotonou, Benin Republic; Mr. Iziak Olaoye formerly of Zico Entertainment; Mr. Babatunde Ahmed Sanni of Silimed Technical Service; Mr. Muideen Buhari of Mubak Wood Technology, Mr. Abdulsalam Abu Salam (sasco) among others numerous to mention for their assistance morally and spiritually.

The reference materials that are contacted for the production need mentioning. I give kudos to the publishers of 'The Punch Newspaper' and Oxford Advanced Learners Dictionary and the social media networks consulted for the research to be worthy of publishing among others.

DEDICATION

The work is dedicated to those who share my philosophy of showing the mono-product nations and institutions, public and private, better and assured path to finance budgets without borrowing through the use of apps to collect taxes and other tariffs from the ministries, departments and agencies.

SYNOPSIS

With the proper implementation of the underlined in the mission statement, of the new ministry of Communications Technology, especially from the improved (in anticipation) level of operation of the powers of NCC whose powers would have created new jobs and increase the level of revenue generations, the communication sector <u>should</u> be the **cash-cow** outwitting such ministries like petroleum, agriculture, solid minerals, works and labour in the **creation of revenues in billions monthly and employment** for the youths in millions. Four aspects that are lacking in the sector are namely social infrastructures especially electricity, content, human capital and mobile infrastructures according to **Prof Umar Garba Danbatta**, the Executive Vice Chairman (EVC) of NCC (The Punch: 2015). These deficiencies call for reforms in the sectors. In order to create human capital for the industry, several private tutors and trainers in all the classes of licenses should be licensed to operate as the tertiary and specialized units in institutions are licensed and registered to operate the relevant Information and Communications Technology (ICT) courses in formal and 'informal' schools to boost the communications sector.

Private investors in electricity generation and distribution must be licensed to operate on the existing distribution, transmission and generation companies. If for instance, a distribution company is limited to distribute <u>three local government areas</u>, the nation would have contracted out not less than **258** for the whole nation. By these steps, thousands of direct jobs would have been created. Through the proposed reforms, more private telecoms investors must be licensed to build mobile and fixed/fixed wireless data infrastructures, software making firms must be licensed with attractive conditions of operations; Several other **reforms** through human-faced regulations from the NCC and the supervisory ministry that would aid security intelligence and social engineering of the nation' growth and development under the change mantra style of governance must be part of the ministry's set target to safeguard the loss of lives and property across the length and breadth of the nation. E-driven strategies with the use of e-platforms should be the major tools to run the systems in this century. By so doing, the status and rating of **Nigeria in the ICT development index would improve from 134 to higher position** in the world (The Punch: 2015). Another solution to the identified challenges facing the sector by the words of the EVC is simply in the building of mobile and internet service infrastructures that would serve the built human capital from schools and institutes and creating enabling operating environment where there is improved data centre solution which would enable the **data centers** to function optimally; software-defined infrastructures are available for the **developers of software** for different business models- profit and charity-based. This would lower the costs and accelerate the time to market for new affiliate services to see the light of the day. It is projected that ICT would contribute one-quarter of the gross domestic products (GDP) by **2025** according to the EVC of NCC, Prof. Umar Garba Danbatta (The Punch: 2015). We are of the opinion that with the reforms suggested in the book, this is attainable with a short space of time of a few months! This is can be seen from simple calculations on how the nation could generate unremitted VATs and corporate sales taxes to the coffers of the government. After all, VAT has been collected from all subscribers at the point of purchase. What stops the licensees to deduct and pay the right amount to the treasury of the environment where they operate? The attitude of not paying the actual sum is financial crime under **tax evasion**.

By the poor and epileptic Quality of Services (QoS) of the voices and data services from the licenses, businesses and people bear the brunt. In banks, many customers lost their hard-earned money to ineffective automated teller machines (ATMs) and **dysfunctional database**. Data gets lost or attacked by cyber virus from **malware**. In transactions, illicit customers who never debited earned from what the original depositors had from accounts. Business and social transactions are slowed down by poor network service for transfer of funds. Hitches in calls at broadcast stations are making adverse effects on the national economic development and growth.

On the part of government that relies heavily on a single product like Nigeria, communications sector can **effectively** replace the petroleum sector to acquire enough to run vital sections of the fiscal budgets. Many nations of the advanced world are reaping billions from the effective use of this sector.

Recently, the nation employed the service of a software firm for the single treasury account on agreement of one-percent. All companies-public and private, are in dire need of one software or the other to develop their staff and working departments. The improved software are needed for the institutions to be at the best of their careers. The need for better software is making the competition keen and the thriving of the software building industry. In fact, the nations in the Europe, Asia and America are investing billions on the communications and technology sector to generate trillions and employment for millions of their citizens. Most of them have empowered their businesses and individuals with improved communication business which birthed ICT. With the ICT innovations and devices, information are always at the fingertips of users and several online-based businesses have taken to the stage and reaping billions as profits. Broadcast media have been tremendously improved upon for dissemination of information to users. Selling of products and services have been improved upon via online selling through online channels. Many self-bosses have emerged and effectively running their businesses. Services delivery has been enhanced. Quality of production has improved tremendously. Research stations are increasing to roll out research works daily and educational products and services are first class. The gains from the communications ministry are no doubt inestimable to the growth and development of the Gross Domestic Products (GDPs) and Gross National Income (GNI).

In Nigeria, the ministry is used to be Ministry of Communications Technology and Information before the separation to give each a separate identity for better productivity. Normally, there is a connection between the two ministries as they have to do with the use of facilities and tools available under them to dissemination of information for nation building. Both could use the professional inputs and technical inputs to have the right statistics and the development of the right technology to eliminate the evaders of taxes no matter how highly placed they are in the nation and outside the nation. This is the main purpose of this research-based book with the use of Nigeria as a case study. All underdeveloped and developing nations that are badly hit by evasion of taxes and other revenues and heavily dependent on a single product shall find the content very irresistible and valuable asset.

Naturally, men started communicating by the natural synergy of his sense organs. Socialization becomes feasible with ease. As generation replaced another on earth, people-of diverse cultures and languages, scribbled down what they intended to communicate as messages and texts. The written texts were usually transported in letters before the era of courier services of the present age. More interestingly, electronic mailing has sent letter writing into the stone-age. People converse more with the applications on mobile phones and laptops. This is faster and easy responded to by the persons involved.

Digital innovation in the communication sector that brought about the use of electronic means is uninterrupted. People, business, institutions *et al.* start to communicate via radio, television, table or desktop phone, mobile phones among several other communication devices through generations of communications innovations. The first generation of innovations otherwise called the 1G saw the advent of the gigabytes. During this time, letters which were sent through post and hand delivered was transferred via telex and fax messages and later via courier and electronic mails. Short Waves medium (SW) and Medium Waves (MW) of broadband was common for the transmission of radio and Very High Frequency (VHF) for television. It was later advanced to Ultra High Frequency (UHF) for television and the Frequency Modulation (FM) for radio stations audio frequency in the later generations. The evolution of General Packet radio Service (GPRS), a wireless data that is readily available to all global system of mobile communication networks (GSM), as part of the 2nd generation of two gigabytes (2G).

In the third (3G) and fourth generations (4G), measurements had expanded the revolution in this sector. Several other users have joined the earliest users and these include the auto-trackers, the security outfits, the Surveyors, Engineers, Architects, the cable media stations, the educational, research and financial institutions.

At the moment, many internet users use both the GPRS and EDGE (Enhanced Data GSM Environment), Universal Mobile telephone Service (UMTS) for to communicate and to go about their daily jobs. In communications parlance, in accordance with the teaching of the noblest among mankind, 'there is no effective communication until the decoder can decode the message of the speaker. Therefore, there is no room for speaker(s) without the listener(s). And the medium of communication or channel known as message conveyers or the links must be right and provided. This is where the communication technologies and interpreters come in with the modern trend of the use of the illustrated 1G, 2G 2.5G for call and text and several other uses in communication sector. The 2.5G is a period between the second generation and the third generation; followed by 3G and 3.5G which caters for internet services. The latest 4G provides extra services for the convenience of the subscribers to reach out with global world with ease and at affordable charges. GPRS complements Bluetooth. The working together, technically, of the stakeholders brings about third generation partnership project (3GPP). In addition to internet Protocol (IP), the technology supports x.25; a packet-based protocol that is used widely in Europe. GPRS is therefore an evolutionary step toward EDGE and UMTS.

Today, the global system of mobile communication association (GSMA) cannot do without the technologies to make business in order to improve the quality of service (QoS) for subscribers at all times and places. With the rapid developments of new innovation to drive communications systems, many professionals and institutions need not to worry about communications like they used to.. At this era of a new generation, probably of 4G, it does not require visiting factories before a job is done. It does not require the presence at the banking halls before financial obligation are met. One good fact about communications is to use the right language for decoder to understand and properly interpret for required actions to take place. A writer who writes with idioms and vocabularies may be speaking to self and not the general public. A reported speech from the lips of the noblest among mankind says that "someone whose speech cannot be decoded is not speaking." Communications must therefore be simple and unambiguous for the **conveyers**, **listeners** and **users** to decode and act upon.

Is communication necessary? Yes, to pass message of instructions, to address an issue for corrective measures or to call to service. When a reporter or a complainant send a message over vandalization of electricity equipment through the radio or television; or such is scripted inside the newspaper, such reporter has called attention of the right authorities to wake up to their responsibility.

Through the ICT facilities, short message services, premium SMS or interactive television (iTV), MMS and broadcast media, online and offline, are available to subscribers at competitive prices. Unfortunately, most do not know the right channels to send the message especially in the modern world when it is easier to use **cyberspace** more than the physical space to send information. This is an era where ideas flow in the cyberspace at a travel of light through advancements in the information and communications technology (ICT). One can say that we are all ignorant of information of the right channels to relay a complaint that would add values to governance and **social engineering** and **technology**. Social networking is easier and several deals can be reached with little cost at the inception of the improved communications sector. People can assess information that were before now inaccessible and could use these platforms to have first-hand information about the situation of issues in the nation and across the worlds.

In retrospect, all sectors, especially communication, ministry, institutions and agencies, must introduce relevant and urgent reforms to make a success and optimal use of resources. The reforms must protect the customers, the operating and the prospective telecoms-related firms and the integrity of the nation where such is needed to portray the right national values to the global market and prospective clients across the globe <u>in a way that both revenues and lucrative jobs shall be generated</u> for the nation especially by the use of special apps from the communication technology to collect all taxes and other revenues from sources. These can only be effective with the right leadership with genuine vision and accomplished mission especially in this change mantra era of leadership.

In conclusion, in the nations where people and institutions evade taxes, the need to call the experts from the communication and information ministry is inevitable where customized apps are created for all the sectors of all the ministries, departments and agencies to have all forms of revenues for the nation deduct at source. There is tendency of loss of jobs for many workers being involved to collect cash and working the amount when a programme by application is doing the job by robots and automated machines using the applications, yet the nation shall have enough to spend as intervention funds to empower several sole proprietor businesses and supporting the SMEs and the large scale industries to expand their manufacturing base. Through the latter, there would be new jobs created and those who lost their jobs to automation programmed to collect the revenues shall be gainfully employed.

CHANGE IS INEVITABLE

Everyone in the nation <u>asks</u> and <u>deserves</u> for change from the old ways as technology moves from analog to digital. The nation deserves a switch from sole dependence on the proceeds from crude oil or a product to other sources especially in the non-oil sectors such as <u>education</u>, <u>sports</u>, <u>tourism</u>, <u>researches</u>, <u>arts</u>, <u>entertainment</u>, <u>publishing</u>, <u>agricultural economy</u> and <u>traditional medicine</u> among others. The nation has very high consumption levels and this is an assurance for high volumes of transactions to spread the wealth. Everyone desires values for their hard-earned money from quality services across boards and not in the communication sector alone but all the other non-oil sectors. Investors in the telecom sectors desire to be more efficient and effective in order to enjoy more patronage from their higher level of reliability by the subscribers along with profits making with ease at peak and off-peak periods.

In this work, we emphasized on the process by which the nation would end borrowing to fund projects and the heavy dependence on the receipts from dwindling forex from the oil sector. And the simple ways for the nation to earn **over one trillion naira on monthly basis** is from the reforming of the process of collecting taxes, VATs and other revenues especially <u>from</u> and <u>through</u> the thriving communications and information sectors in the nation. The anticipated reforms must start from putting the round pegs on the round holes. And the next is the employment of ICT gurus to produce domiciled apps for all the sources of revenues and the sensitization of all the payers on the new ways to pay without the cash by the use of internet-based devices. Through the urgent and steady processes of reforms where all the bottlenecks of bureaucratic systems are removed, the regulations of relevant institutions in the sector are revisited and properly reviewed; relevant amendments to legislations establishing the affiliates of the ministry are to be urgently re-amended, the **mobile and internet infrastructures** must be provided in a larger scale and better enabling environment is created for all stakeholders-investors-new and local, affiliates, customers and the regulatory bodies; by so doing, wealth is created and distributed and lucrative and decent jobs would also be created for millions of idlers and hardworking bloggers.

Conclusively, on the part of the subscribers to the networks providers, government could generate revenues from fines over infringement on their rights to quality service. They used to have complaints over poor services, unsolicited messages, fraudulent deductions on unsubscribe services and products such as caller tunes, automatic data plan not solicited for, unfair and discrepancies in service charges, long time of connections, total disconnects and loss of signals and services among several others must be looked into. Several complaints of the subscribers are met without responses from the regulatory authority save a few instances when the operators are fined to pay to the coffers of the government while the customer receive no financial or credits/bytes compensation. Therefore, it is apparent that government supervising ministry and the regulatory agencies are only after the taxes and levies as penalty on the networks and not for the customers in their millions.

IT IS EASY TO CREATE OVER ONE TRILLION MONTHLY FROM COMMUNICATIONS SECTOR WITH APPS FOR COLLECTIONS

Budget of the nation runs into about six or seven trillion under the present regime but it is always a deficit budget. Where should the nation get the excess to fund the budget after realizing part from the oil sector? Should it go borrowing with stringent conditions attachable by the creditors to fund laudable projects that would impact lives and transform institutions? This is the message to the nation and those nations running mono-product economy. The products and services from this sector are adequate to turn the sector into major source of revenues to the coffers of the nation much like Japan. The rate of growth of the sector operators and subscribers are high. Statistics confirm that the subscriptions of the firms grow by **11,517,021** or **7.443%** between December 2014 and the 3rd quarter of 2015 when the subscribers grow from **139,143,610** to **150,660,631**.

Out of this, **over 98%** are on mobile GSM, **1.36%** on mobile CDMA and **0.12%** for fixed/fixed wireless (NCC: 2015).Another source claimed that Nigeria, with the largest mobile market in Africa, has 107% penetration and of about 148 million subscribers (Buddie.com: 2015). The rapid growth of subscriptions of ever increasing demand for bandwidths is traced to be one of the major causes of network congestion and poor services. From the growing rate of subscriptions and the degree of consumption of the subscribers-regardless of their status and income distributions, the nation can generate both revenues and employments from the sector. Studies confirm that subscribers engage in **calls, browsing of internets, uploading of materials** and **downloading of e-materials** including: **songs, films, documentaries, videos,** game **results, books** and **statistical information for research stations**. This service is also utilized by several other professional users in communications like the courier service and logistics, the transport sector particularly the aviation, the seaports; the online and convectional media stations (print or electronic)and several other users. **Software developers;** individuals and firms, cannot do without internet services and data to run efficiently and effectively. Several smartphones (androids, iphones, ipads) and blackberry phone users pay for data subscriptions as they desire or could afford to pay for. Our studies show that the nation is being shortchanged in the payment of taxes especially the value added taxes (VATs) for all the **purchases** and **payments** for all contractual activities of investments in the sector and for subscribers' subscriptions.

Towards positivity and turning the sector into **cash-cow**, inadequate information and fraudulently doctored records of patronages from the licensed firms under the sector do a lot of damage to the treasury. We would give several ways by which our **two-pronged objectives** (wealth and employment creation) could be easily met. Let us use a few mathematical illustrations on how to generate incomes for the nation from the procurement of **credits for calls** only. Mathematically, assuming **one hundred million** are active **post-paid** subscribers to all the mobile networks use an average of **200 naira calls** per week, the nation should be expected to make **400 x 200 million naira per month** amounting to **80 billion naira per month**. **10%** Value-Added-Tax which includes the withholding taxes alone would amount to **8billion naira per month** from **post-paid** clients who are students, artisans and below average-living people like the rural dwellers, the illiterate market men and women.

Truth be told, the above calculation is a child-play but serves as an eye-opener to the estimable **tax evasion** in form of already charged and collected 10% VAT on each card sold to the subscribers at different times and places. We mean that the estimation above is a far cry considering the number of credits that are being used by **pre-paid** rich and affluent Nigerians and non-Nigerians that run into several tens and hundreds of thousands altogether in addition with their family members, business associates, clubs members and friends per month. Studies show that many rich subscribers to the pre-paid call plans spend several tens of thousands naira per month which they earn awards for patronage. Rich **pre-paid subscribers** could make calls to the tune of over two hundred thousand naira per month with the freebies in megabytes for other internet uses instead of buying **data bundles**. To the MNOs, selling credits with free megabytes is a selling strategy as it is an indirect selling of both products for the target subscribers. An average and below average **Nigerian post paid subscribers** can talk for not less than **5 hours in a week** making **60 x 5= 300 minutes** when per minute (PM) call varies from network to network and **peak** and **off-peak periods** by our rough estimations based on the criteria like the subscribers' preferences and interest, the switch over from one network to the other if one fails to deliver quality service, preference of certain networks for different purpose et al. Some users are given networks by their companies as the company's own network based on agreement with the operators; some prefer certain network for the reach and easy connection at different places. With certain codes and guides, a subscriber could buy available credits of other networks and change the credits to his own network (where he subscribed). **Mobile Number Portability** (MNP) otherwise called 'Porting' (switching loyalty) from a network to another, without necessarily changing the number of the former, is easy by the operators for the subscribers. All these, though, are for a service charge. On these bases, they load credits on all the available networks on their phones at all times. This is enough confirmation that no subscriber that drops a network would reduce the number of the subscribers. And the level of consumptions may vary time to time and place to place, event to event. Studies show that people buy data to run official works in offices and call credits are bought at the weekends more than in the ordinary days. As regards the **degree of consumptions** (subscriptions), let us assume an average of **.35 naira** per second billing (average mean of the minimum **0.20** at the off-peak periods and maximum **0.50 naira** at peak periods being charged from network to network and network to other network), we would have **(.35 x 300 x 60) equals to 6300 naira per week**. If we use this rough estimate to calculate the actual earnings of the mobile network operators of **over 100 million**, we have **6300 x 100 million** making **630 billion naira** as revenues from sales of credits **per week; 10% VAT** would amount to **63billion naira** multiplied by **4 weeks** in a month equals **252 billion naira Value Added Tax** **(VAT)** on credits sold per monthly from calls alone (mobile and GSM land or desktop phone). No account of data sold and of all the services being rendered by the operators to different licensed and unlicensed users within and outside the shores with permission from the NCC, the regulatory body and the supervising communications ministry.

Calls	Network	Network	period	per second billing		
	M t n	M t n	off-peak	2	0	k
	M t n	G l o	Offpeak	5	0	k

Average charge equals 35k as our price to multiple of the minimum call period in seconds per week. This could cause disputes from conflicting facts and figures from the stakeholders in the sector and thereby generate academic exercises without thorough **reforms** (urgent surgery) of the sector and the powers that established the regulatory body, NCC.

Critical studies apparently confirm that the number of SIM cards being used for **mobile** and **landline** calls from the licensed mobile network operators is more than **200 million**. We mathematically showed in the book though the active users are put at approximation of **146 million** by the NCC even though the third quarter of 2015 shows that **148,427,043** are subscribers for the major four mobile operators namely MTN, Globalcom mobile or Globacom, Airtel, Etisalat now

9mobile. Those (individuals, businesses, institutions...) who use their credits and data to make calls, sending SMS, MMS, watching cable and terrestrial television and videos, on phones, laptops and related electronic devices; browse for information, researching for data, uploading, downloading of books, films, songs, documentaries, events..) with the use of data are increasing by the day as shown earlier. More are into mobile browsing with GSM and CDMA with the use of the highly patronage mobile devices (phones, tablets, laptops, androids...) than patronizing any available business cafe. Studies confirm that customers make purchases every minute of the day. Those who are too poor to buy credits and data like the students, the aged people living in the cities, towns, villages, the retirees, the pensioners used to have generous relatives and close relations who buy for them gratis periodically. It is an established fact that all subscribers used to have credits on their phones for personal uses. If we use rough estimates of **80 million** of **data** users among the active subscribers to the four popular networks, and we assumed only **seven thousand naira** of **data** is the **average** for all categories of users (rich and poor, working or retired, students and tutors, business and non-business, government and non-government) in **a week**; we would therefore have **80 million multiply by 28,000 naira per month** as incomes to the telecom operators. This amounts to **2,240,000 million naira** which would give **224 billion naira** 10% **VAT per month**!

It is common today that a very large percentage of classes of browsers buy data as they buy credits to make calls and engage in light internet services like opening of emails, reading of newspaper, social media chats. Let us consider how much it will cost the website developers, the software developers, the ICT-based services in IT-enhanced markets where manual jobs have become software-based where digital transformation is the vogue, intercom for business and other institutions (educational, logistics and courier services, media business especially digital businesses, research stations for different sectors of economy, financial, professional, religious). If we add up the amounts of VAT of credit cards and the tariffs of data plans, we would at least have a whopping sum of **224 + 252** making **476 billion naira per month**! This is an **achievable** rough estimation from the sector on monthly basis. Our studies show that the nation could get the higher figures from the revelation at a chapter in the book. Under the chapter, we critically examine the subscribers by market segmentations, the purchases as shown in the **tables** and other clients of the products and services from the **licensees** in the sector.

In retrospect, one can imagine what they make in several other services being provided by the MNOs and how much they could make if the <u>economy is booming</u> and the <u>political system is stable</u>. What about the VATs on short message service, data sales of gigabytes and megabytes for browsers in retail and bulk. It is a fact that bulk message senders procure choice and affordable data plans from the operators at a cheap price in other to sell at a profit, video-conferencing, shooting and transfer of documents, photo-shots services from data service providers as all MNOs are also into **voice** and **data services**, money and credit transfers, utility bills payments. Is it not due to have right estimates of all other forms of payable taxes; corporate tax, sales tax, personal income tax that must be paid into the coffers of Federal Inland Revenue Service (FIRS) from the sector licensed operators?

With the combination of the call **credits** and **data** with different tariffs being purchased by **pre-paid** and **post-paid** customers and subscribers at **retail** and **wholesale** levels from different firms selling and operating with the voice and data services, **subscribers** can be estimated to run to several hundreds of million above the estimates. And the rough revenues of the operators could run to the tune of **over One Trillion naira per month** as later shown on some tables Mathematically. By the revelations in this book, all 'secretly' kept records to track the sales of all the licensed operators and get all the necessary taxes and dues from the firms would be unveiled and become a public discourse. <u>The regulatory agencies and the supervisory ministry could understand that truly the earnings from the sector are enough to run the fiscal budgets without proceeds from crude oil</u>. The heavy reliance would be a thing of the past if the suggested **reforms** are studied and fully implemented. If the nation is not earning as much from the call credits purchases alone as VAT, then it has been shortchanged and **measures** should be taken to redress the abnormality and illegality as we have at the tail end of this book. Certain inevitable **reforms** must be carried out with the powers bestow on the Nigerian Communications Commission (NCC) under the **Section 3**, of **2003** of the Nigerian Communications Act (NCA) towards receiving the accumulated taxes or deduction from the source (points of purchases).

In the light of the above, to make target revenues from the purported reforms, it is a pointer and confirmation that advanced nations like **United Kingdom** relies so much on the taxes because of the huge funds that can be generated at the source with ease. The advanced nations use the same **communications technology e-solutions** and **devices** to get the right taxes from the sources to reducing tax evasion to the minimum possible as a result of adequate profile from the people to avoid tax evasion. This nation must not be an exemption especially at this time when the prices of oil is crashing every day in world oil market. The proceeds would grow the other sectors through dependable **reforms** to prevent the **tax evaders** under the guise of multiple taxations and flimsy excuses. The **reforms** would also check the producers and users of **malicious ware** (malware) in the nation and encourage the builders of relevant software for all the sectors of the economy. People's contribution towards the realization of the **reforms** would determine how effective and efficient such would have on the nation's integrity. If those managing each unit are insincere and grossly irresponsible to duty, erupting slow bureaucratic problem would crush the objective and render all efforts fruitless at outset. In view of all these, **trouble-shootings** are identified with causes and practicable solutions. We eventually invent **five-pronged reforms** for the stakeholders in the chapter four of the book.

In fact, with the appropriate mobile and internet structures for the ICT firms under the management of technical staff that are of quality breed, versatile and creative, the nation would save a lot of money, and institutions and businesses from ruins. Many fraudulent internet service providers and the **mobile networks operators** whose sites and assets are being used to commit illicit acts can be retrained from criminal activities especially **economic** and **financial crimes**.

THE FINAL NOTES

It is highly feasible to run transparent government and institutions with the contribution of the citizens or workers through the channels created and creatable by the **communications and information sector** especially in the tackling the crimes (kidnapping, fuel hoarding to create artificial scarcity, insecurity to the nation, fire and accidents, illicit inducements, abuses of rights in all forms). We emphasize much on the innovations from the communication technology simply because it is the driver that would drive al other sectors towards huge revenue generation enough to fund laudable projects. Communication is simply a medium by which people (stakeholders within Nigerian and in diaspora) can share their views with the debating bills at national and state assembly even the federal executive council meetings. We can also referred it to as information dissemination. The two sectors work in synergy to create avenues by which people and institutions would send their views, comments, opinions directly and indirectly to the assembly for those on the hot-seat to debate upon. Let us take an instance. State government held a forum where how to improve the earnings from IGR was being discussed. Many people outside may have genuine ways to increase the internally generated incomes. Such should be able to reach out to the forum live through open lines and site for live transmission. This is one of the **socio-economic functions** identified in this book. Through regulation of the active participants in the sector, several software build locally could be exported like other intellectual property to the outside nations. Locally, innovative and specialized software would elevate the **e-learning solutions** for education, agricultural services, security business and financial transactions among others to improve on service delivery and add more to the GDP and GNI for improved **per capita income**. With these reforms, the institutions and stakeholders would be more active towards generating billions from sales tax from evaders with the **apps** from the factories of the apps makers from licensed software makers across the nation. Through effectiveness of the active stakeholders, public and private, **e-fraud** activities of internet scammers would be effectively tackled headlong to minimize the gains anticipated from the e-commerce activities and the development in the communication sector. The

MNOs accuse the VAS of illegality against the subscribers. **Ozioma Ubabukoh**, a journalist with The Punch newspaper wrote that "Subscribers lose 360 billion naira yearly to unsolicited SMS (Saturday Punch, Nov; 21, 2015, page 57) National association of telecommunications subscribers of Nigeria complain that at least 200 million naira are lost monthly, if we use the **200 million benchmark** of all Subscriber Identity Mobile (SIM) cards for all mobile and MODEM users combined, they lost **40 billion naira** in a month and **480 billion naira** in a year! What about the incomes that can be generated from the licensed users for internet-based business purposes as in the cafes, schools, research stations, media, security institutions, financial institutions and the numerous professional institutes licensed to operate certain classes of the telecoms jobs to increase the human capital capacity and for the building new contents of modern tastes and needs? If these institutes and businesses are collated and relevant levies are collected as enshrined in the powers of the Nigerian Communications Commission (NCC) to regulate and inspect the licensees' books of accounts by **Section 3 of the NCC act of 2003** of the **Nigerian Communications Act (NCA)**. This huge money could be refunded to the coffers of the government and the subscribers get their dues refunded in form of **free credits** if necessary steps are taken as revealed as part of the **reforms** in this book.

From MNOs records, there are **nine licensees** of mobile networks operating both voice (calls) and data services (internet browsing and other services). **Unhealthy promotions** (which would be part of revelations in the book) that are not checked by the helms of affairs do not stem the tide. The sector must not be monopolized by a few firms. A big market like Nigeria should have not less than twenty licensed and effectively operational MNOs and several internet service providers for private and business uses under different classes of categorization in the NCC powers of issuing licenses.

With the license of new operators, several thousands of lucrative jobs from e-commerce activities from different forms of **innovations** would be employed and wealth will be evenly distributed. Direct effects on the effectiveness and efficiency of the postal and other telecommunication services would be great in the increase in the Gross Domestic Product (GDP) and Gross National Income (GNI).

In fact, the proliferation of e-commerce, e-trading, e-forex, e-governance, e-solutions, e-learning and limitless use of internet services would boost the **liberalization of communications sector** especially the dying postal services. More private **courier services** with different <u>creativity and versatility</u> would spring up across the nation. Distribution and other logistics services would be positively impacted and thousands of jobs would be directly and indirectly created as wealth is being circulated. One can imagine the circulation of **billions of naira per month** from the sector in the nation and number of proliferation of affiliate jobs from expansion of the licensees. Those who lost their jobs to automation machines at different institutions especially in the collection of revenues (taxes, duties, rates, licenses..) would have new jobs from the support of special intervention funds for the SMEs and the large scale business by the government. The cycle is to eternity. What a big impact in stability such would have on the socio-economic life of the nation.

Generally speaking, communication devices and enhancements (infrastructures) are inevitable to connect man to man, place to place, government to government, business to business and institutions to institutions. In the working of administration, it is vital. The **executive arms of government** must communicate with the legislature and the judiciary to make political administration work at the instance of working policies for all the sectors. The rank and file of the security agencies must enjoy effective communications to be effective in their performance to enforce laws and orders. Population commission cannot do without the database collection and monitoring for the planning and budget department of government; the schools must have records of the staff members and students in database; the immigration service must have adequate knowledge of the number of emigrants and the immigrants; the hospitals must forward all the records of births and deaths to the population commission to keep the data for national planning on health infrastructures as this would enable the government to be aware of the planned or proposed fiscal budgets on **deficits** or **surplus** of health super and infrastructures; the courts must have central aside the local database where all records of cases and dispensation of justices are kept for references.; the security forces are in dire need of information and data of people, business, institutions... to be able to enforce laws and orders. <u>It would not be difficult to identify law breakers</u> from records from all the relevant agencies and ministries. This reminds me a criminal issue. Somebody called a close pal with a network number. He made some demands on phone which the person obliged to out of empathy. She got to know later that the man had stolen by trick. He had defrauded her of a lump sum of money. I told her not to panic as all relevant information about the man must be with service provider. Through some legal processes, we got in touch with the provider to track the offender. We took this path as we had tracked a kidnapped person through the last calls he made through the mobile network operators of his. In several cases, it may be difficult if all the users are not properly registered with the operators.

Today, with such input like Bank Verification Number (BVN), driver's license registration, the national identity card and voter's card registration in different portals, majority of the nationals and non-nationals have no hidden place. All faces can be unveiled with little stress.

In retrospect, if all schools, health institutions, business institutions (manufacturing, processing, wholesaling, retailing and service-oriented) across the nation are mandated by law to have database office where all daily records are kept and those of the elements (staff, equipment, and facilities) within, then the nation would be more productive as security challenges may be nipped in the bud and the amount of working hours being lost would be used for productive purposes. And the effective and efficient governance would be achieved with all the aforementioned connecting and supplying the weekly information to the central database of the nation. Many benefits, this process, would serve the nation in the planning and budgeting. With ease, government can be aware of the number of graduates with different courses per year or academic session as regards planning ahead for employments creation or provision after service; government would know the actual number of health facilities that are in short supply in the hospitals across the nation; the number and the original nations of migrants shall be known for security planning and networking.

WARNING SHOT

The peculiarity of the stakeholders in different operating business environment really matters. A poor nation cannot afford to embrace the strategy of collecting taxes and other revenues from the rich nation hook, line and sinker. The people vary from clime to clime since their orientation about the nation and life differs. Developed nations like the United States of America (USA), China, Britain and Germany et al. all have different ways to regulate the activities of all firms in the telephony sector and all internet-based firms towards earning the right amount of taxes and other revenues. They have developed the right technology and strategies to track the taxable persons and items, online and offline. The fear of adding fuels into fire is major on the loss of jobs of the citizens if they should replace collecting by hand with the collecting through automation machine. Doing the former is better if the gains are weigh side by side. A government who has right and practicable employment policy should be able to boost the employment market with large chunk of the realized taxes especially in the reinvesting huge funds from the taxes and other revenues realized through the automation for capital projects across the nation. In America by research findings, Federal Trade Commission (FTC) regulates the activities of the **e-commerce** such as the **amazon.com** and barnesandnobles.com. China uses stricter legal frameworks to regulate what is placed and sold on internet cyber space in order to reflect the national interest.

On the negative side, internet has become a major pathway to internet crimes and frauds by the criminal elements regardless of status, gender, affiliations, educational qualification and ethno-religion status. It is reported that internet banking fraud is the highest crime in United Kingdom according to **guardian.com** (The Punch, December 1, 2015 page 14). It is easy for hackers, certified and non-certified, to pilfer into private accounts likewise the unregistered 'value added service' operators that have negative intents such as stealing or adulteration of data and valuable security-related information especially to serve as spies or committing economic and financial crimes. Influential individuals and institutions among the tax evaders and several other legal and illegal institutions that are into e-solutions can develop anti-software to scale down the workings of the original software. Those who develop virus to attack systems and portals use the knowledge from the ICT which is a product of developed communications technology. With this in mind, the ministry of communications and its agency, the Nigerian Communications Commission (NCC), have a lot to do to with their powers to **reforms** the listed functions and making the objectives realizable in order to protect the national interests via promoting the national values in the products and services being placed on internet simply to avoid erosion of national norms and values; encourage the adding of more values to the capacity building of the software makers locally to produce what are at first needed in software to <u>drive the local knowledge-driven economy</u> useful to track all forms of taxes especially <u>deducting the VATs</u> at source. The topmost priority is aimed at protecting locally-based e-commerce ventures registered and hence promoting emergence of IT-related markets and specialized institutions where ICT graduates are produced en masse in Nigeria.

To protect and encourage the licensees, the affiliates like the phone making industry, the sellers of credits and data (wholesale and retail) and the buyers in retail or bulk too must protect the financial institutions and government from all forms of **e-frauds** and nip corruption in the bud through cash rewarding **i-reportings** from all sources. Billions are generated to the coffers of the nation from tracked taxes especially VATs as the firms expand to accommodate new employees in thousands. The think-tank employed must think ahead of dupers!

Conclusively, unlike crude-oil that has several alternatives, communication has no alternatives. <u>Everyone</u> (individual, business and political institutions, educational and medical institutions) at all times and all places must communicate through one medium or another. Every person and business (government and non-government) desires to get their message passed to the right recipient (s) within the twinkle of an eye and not at the snail speed like in the ancient times. The advancement in the sector has become the solutions to ensure these desires at a good cost (pricing, availability and timing). Therefore, there are inevitable institutional reforms in form of dynamic challenges facing the sector. In-depth elaboration of these are contained in a chapter in this book. However, these challenges include:

a) Creating enabling operating environment which synergize the stakeholders' contributions towards building effective and steadily improving communications sector as a driver to all other sectors where the contributions of the associations like the Nigerian Computer Society (NCS), ALTON, NATCOMS with the mission of NCC under the supervisory activities of the Ministry of communications to achieve overall results are inevitable
b) Synergize the operators through effective and regulated interconnectivity targeted at ensuring affordable costs of services to the people and businesses
c) Ensuring that reliable broadband for operators and working infrastructures are at the beck and call of the users and at affordable procurement costs with increasing investments to boost the service delivery
d) Encouraging the synergy to move the nation into advanced economy through collaboration with MDAs like the Ministry of Defence, Ministries of Education and Science and Technology in the pursuant of technical careers by students for the generation for both wealth and jobs from the sector.
e) Protecting the consumer privacy and rights especially to halt extortions from the licensees in the telecom and postal sectors when there is dire need for security reason and avoiding infringements on certain rights such as the electrical, mechanical and patent rights of the makers and operators as recognized by laws.
f) Synergize the ministerial activities of the ministries and change the system of governance under the new **change mantra** to protect the national integrity, safe lives and property and keep every institution, persons, associations and agencies on their toes through network coordination and distribution of facts.
g) Monitoring of all MNOs towards rendering effective and efficient services to their subscribers and to supervise the data in databases with back-ups to avoid data loss in all the affiliate units and agencies.

h) Tracking the unregistered Value Added Service (VAS) providers and other licensees shortchanging the subscribers illegally.
i) Tracking the taxes of the operators and several online or internet-based businesses and unpaid dues for the coffers of the government through our prescribed solutions simply to avoid tax evasion from all various forms of subscriptions of the millions of subscribers
j) Monitoring and supervising the advertising regulations via working with the relevant agencies such as APCON, AAAON et al and those of the data services providers and users
k) Build a more effective and efficient postal services including the licensing and regulating the involvement of more courier services across the length and breadth of the nation
l) Use the experts in the communications technology to create apps suitable to have the data of houses, people by what they earn, the industries and institutions operating in the nation to be able to have the real figure of the taxable items and collection of the actual revenues deductible at source. If for instance, the number of the structures (houses, offices, hotels, fuel stations, schools, hospitals, malls, others) are known, the actual amount of VAT on the electricity supply shall be collected.
m) And the general gain is to save the nation from borrowing, locally and internationally, to finance capital and recurrent expenditure in the fiscal budget particularly at this period of dwindling crude oil revenues

COMMUNICATIONS AND INFORMATION TECHNOLOGY MUST PIVOT DIVESTMENT INTO NON-OIL SECTORS TOWARDS REPLACING THE HEAVY DEPENDENCE ON OIL RECEIPTS

Man uses information to develop products and services. The information about a nation propels the need to research into solutions for identified challenges. Recalling economic history, Nigeria has been a **mono-economy** for several years traced back to the crude oil boom of 70's. The nation apparently relegated the agricultural economy business for the revenues being generated from oil aftermath the agricultural economy that had sustained the regions for years. At the moment, crude oil sales have become a source of worry to a major marketer of the mineral resources across the nation by the dwindling prices at the world market for several reasons of international agenda. There is economic recession moving in swiftly earlier than expected. And this has created rooms for thinkers to come out with other sources of raising revenues to sustain the economy, build more and maintain the infrastructures. The administration of **'change mantra'** of the ruling party in Nigeria at the moment (2015-2019) has opened the chances for the thinkers on all the sectors of the economy to produce blueprints towards boosting the nation's economy and resuscitate all other areas that would enhance employment creation for the millions who are unemployed especially among the youths. Such areas of divestment is the heavy investment on ICT to power the rest of the sectors. Communications and information infrastructures must be birthed by the administration to improve on all other sectors. A glaring fact is that many advanced nations generate huge wealth and create millions of direct and indirect jobs through knowledge-based economy courtesy of the advancing innovations in the communications sector rather than heavy reliance on mineral resources from the belly of the earth (land). More money is made on air than what they generate from soil. In such advancing economy, they feed the mouths and the manufacturing base from the produce from soil and the innovations from the air is connecting the people and institutions to grow the sectors altogether. The communications innovations assist the farmers in all the farms to have relevant information on farm practices to ensure large scale production in order to feed the people and keep the agro-allied industries and the livestock growing for their **multiplier ripple effects** on the overall domestic products of the nation. The question is "How does the advanced nation turn the communications sector into cash-cows?"

It is very simple. They invest in the development of the technology since communications technologies connect everyone (persons, institutions, government departments and agencies…), attach **stiff punitive measures against tax evaders** and it also determines the volumes of trades and transaction aside saving time and money; they also provide and keep investing to ensure a sustainable growth of the sector. This is making available all needed social internet infrastructures and friendly but business-oriented **regulations** through relevant agencies of the activities of the operating firms through different agencies and institutions through having full control over the users by records keeping for tracking purposes.

With this, all forms of **intellectual resources** are legally sold or illegally downloaded free online, software firms are gradually taken over the business environment. In the nation today, not less than **31 software firms** are top earners according to **nairaland site** (Nairaland: 2015). Several logistics and courier services, media entrepreneurs and digital or tech-preneurs are proliferating. All these have the internet services and value-added products (**megabytes, kilobits, gigabytes**) and of services as materials to build their products and launch their services to the target subscribers. From all these **purchases**, one can imagine the income that can be generated from Value Added Taxes (VATs) and other forms of taxes and levies. The overall gains are reflected in the smooth running of the **e-administration** or the **e-system** of governance. Earning legitimately from declared right amount of VATs on goods, investments and purchases in the sector, the deduction of company sales tax and pay as you earn (PAYE) taxes from the employees cannot be seen as **multiple taxations**. Companies, institutions and individuals especially contractors hide under this to evade legislated taxes.

Unfortunately, most of those taxes, particularly the **VAT** and the **PAYE** have been deducted from the source.

In retrospect, it is high time Nigeria taken a cue from the ICT-based economic advanced nations to rise from the third world nation to the latter (first world nations) to monitor the sales, collate and collect all the taxes for the building of the nation as the international practices.

SUMMARY

This research-based project is target at the two-pronged issue of **generating due incomes** and thereby eliminates tax evasion. The nation and the nationals become the beneficiaries of <u>collection of actual taxes</u> in order to properly implement the **fiscal budgets** with lucid, unambiguous manner. We show, from our field studies, the practicable mathematical calculations to get the right amount of highlighted different **taxes** especially <u>VATs</u> from the licensed and unregistered but operating telecoms-related firms, lottery and game firms, individual telecoms' licensed/registered contractors/investors and institutions and creating lucrative **employment** for millions through the use of **NCC powers**. By these powers, there are inevitable **practicable reforms,** to make the optimal use of the costly communications and information infrastructures, that must be legally enforced, most probably by national assembly (NASS) legislation, to instill disciplines and correct the institutional ills that have crippled the telecommunications industry for long. This has to be effectively and efficiently accomplished with the inputs of the leadership of the communications ministry in collaboration with other relevant ministries and agencies or institutions. **We finally submit, based on the analyses of our findings, that the new Ministry of Communications is cash cow to the nation from this moment provided all the guides in the book are strictly adhere to as a scripture**. This is the author's contribution to the growth and development of the nation, 'great nation, great people' in the words of the great Nigerian **Professor Dora Akunyili** (of blessed memory) brand of the nation.

PART ONE
WHAT IS COMMUNICATIONS TECHNOLOGY?

Communications technology is undoubtedly the most efficient and cost effective way of passing information and interactions. There would not be effective and efficient information of and from all sectors without communication innovations and devices. Effective broadcasting of messages is a function of working facilities of communications and regulations. It is ancient and remains modern till eternity. In addition, the information about the difficulty to collect revenues catalyzed the innovations to helping in better communication and the use of the devices to collect the revenues.

In the ancient, people communicate through **oral** and later by hand written **letters** delivered by hands. Transporters are the conveyers of such messages which usually took days or months to get replies. Some core traditionalists send messages through certain **symbols** or indigenous **materials**. They listened to gramophone radio at village square. Later, transistor radio of Short and Medium Waves band (SW/MW) and black and white television became a rave affordable by the rich among them. Analog phone was introduced and only a few who could afford the latest innovations; land-phone and desktop phones. At the moment, the nation is going digital which is fast embraced by the consumers.

In today's world, one can cycle the world over in minutes while comfortably seated in a chair or strolling the streets. Man talks face to face with the use of video calls. It is easy to have the names of the caller through true-caller application in mobile phones. Surveillance camera is so tiny that it is now of the components of movable items as small as a biro, eye glasses, buttons not to talk of androids, smartphones among others. The world has indeed reduced to a small global village compared to what it used to be. Through the modern ways of communicating, products of information and communications technology are of different generations. Let us simplify this further. Two gigabytes (**2G**) of the **second generation** communications technology is enough for call and texts. Three gigabytes (**3G**) of **third generation** innovations gives extra broadband service in internet facility with GPRS, EDGE and UMTS technologies and the latest four gigabytes (**4G**) of the **fourth generations** in the communications technology moves subscribers to the next world of communications.

In the business world, operators try to edge out one another with their advanced communications technology-creating equipment. This is as a result of increased productions of software for different users. This we call software evolution and revolution. Some use GPRS, HSDPA and EDGE for the GSM-900; some add MHz UMTS, DS-HSPA+ to the above for operations.

The gain remains that people and businesses can easily communicate with the vitality to the sector through advanced ICT. Through video-conferencing, meetings are held saving the people and institutions huge sum of logistics expenses. Researchers do not need to travel a distance before data and vital information are got from internet. Gone are the days of our ancient forefathers when communications by letters and symbols took many months to get to the destination. An electronic mail or text on phone takes a few seconds to deliver unless the recipient does not have an active **internet connection.** If a business throws its messages (promotions, product campaigns or branding) products and services to the internet, within five minutes, everyone on internet site who click into the site or affiliate to the Search Engine Optimizations (SEOs) would see the content straightaway. Again, effective communications saves lives through reduction in the mass movement of human traffic and those of products; by this, it saves invaluable time and valuable assets.

BENEFICIARIES OF COMMUNICATIONS AND INFORMATION TECHNOLOGY ADVANCEMENTS

Information is sent through effective communication. Communication is effective through the provision of the right communication infrastructures and strong regulatory institutions. Men and institutions need to communicate information, that would impact lives and kick start innovations that would transform words into products and services, time to time just as we need air to breathe. Communications in business makes a success of the business. The hierarchical flow of information is a means of communications that would spur people to task towards meeting the objectives of the business. However, not only individuals and businessmen need communication technology. Many other users include:

a) The software or applications developers
b) Website and blogs developers
c) Information officers like the public relation officers, media team
d) The business institutions like banks, schools, business cafes, mobile money firms, games and lottery firms, money transfer businesses or bureau de change
e) Private and public companies particularly the media stations-convectional and cable under the mass media like the print, broadcasting and electronic or digital media
f) Individuals (entrepreneurs, students, workers, retirees, pensioners, tourists, professionals like the architects, the surveyors, the geologists, the auto makers, the security outfits, the sailors and pilots, entrepreneurs...)
g) Research stations and institutions (security institutions, regulatory institutions, political institutions, bureau of statistics, population or census office, educational and health care institutions for the advancement in the economic, political, social, scientific, technological, spiritual...)

There are some who enter into the communications technology to defraud other people sources of their livelihood. These include the hackers entering into accounts illegality to spy and steal, the internet fraudsters who pretend to be looking for soul mates and marriage, adulterators, impersonators, internet bank pilferers and intellectual thieves who do illegal downloads of intellectual property infringing on the copyright and patent rights of the owners for no charge.

In the light of the above, we can easily say without contradictions that everybody; business, institutions, professional bodies, places no matter the level of literacy and development are subscribers to those who are in the transmission business mobilizing equipment and manpower resources to provide effective means of communications for them at a charge.

.

FUNCTIONS OF COMMUNICATIONS AND INFORMATION TECHNOLOGY TO NATIONAL DEVELOPMENT

All along, we have shown the inevitability of communications. Factually, communication is inevitable to all creatures to ensure **social engineering and technology**. Information is the message that is passed across from one entity to the other with both of them having adequate knowledge of the message. It is information about a people, a nation, an event, an institution, an administration, a product, a service among others. This is the reason for the **synergy** between Information and Communications Technology (ICT). The devices to communicate bring about the innovations that make the sector to be inevitable to all people, businesses and institutions.

For better classification, we shall look at some peculiar functions of communications in the nation. We shall classify the **functions** under social, economic, political, technological functions. Professional associations, individual entrepreneurs and applicants use Linkedin; several sites are for creating social, political and economic friendships and dating. It is a natural wisdom endowed creatures meant to bring them together for a productive and social integration with proper regulations to avoid treason-traced communication. In the light of the above, all creatures communicate with different means and medium.

SOCIAL FUNCTIONS

Today, communications, among men from different races and values, brings about effective and efficient socio-economic integration and development in making businesses advance and profitable under social engineering. When professionals talk, they talk business. One can listen and view, present and contribute to events and issues, local and international, from the comforts of homes and offices after proper connections and paying for the subscriptions, as and when due.

For social interactions, radio and television stations can receive contributions from the listeners and viewers unlike before. Many make connect to old friends, create new ones, date and could end up in blissful marital life through the platform created by this sector especially from social media platforms like facebook, twitter, instagram, whatsapp et al. This has made the share views on issues and proffer solutions to problems and challenges.

Acculturation is made possible through communication. It is easy for induction purposes with the communications devices and the channels of communications. People, of diverse backgrounds and different leanings in life, easily have knowledge of other people's cultural values through socialization for toleration of ethnics. The internet-savvy youths, even the introverts, have found the internet to catch fun as they are able to chat with different minds across the world. Through the facilities, people secure lucrative jobs and business opportunities from internet searching through blogs, personal websites and emails. Browsing websites and blogs is like flying around to coordinate with people and places to achieve set results enhancing **social engineering** and **technology** via improved level of socialization promotions. The publicists or Public Relations Officers of all government and associations are efficient through the presence of communications devices. Certain confidential messages are sent through this secure medium.

All institutions, formal and informal, religion or non-religion, are effective in service delivery and meeting targets via improved communications technology. Gone are the days when letters are opened and read before they got to the receivers despite its lateness to the receiver(s). The electronic world has created better ways to send messages via other means that most secrets can be hidden via coding of messages, photos, vital documents and the use of medium that would protect the content. Today, one can distinguish between the messages and the messengers.

From a social view, the **Mobile Number Portability** (MNP) has created avenues for the keeping the number of the overall subscribers to the MNOs. This 'portability' is an avenue where the subscribers who is dissatisfied with the services of the first operator switch over to the choice one that can provide better quality service. Many use the medium to mobilize people into action and political struggle against anti-people policies of governments.

With the aid of the innovations from the ICT, crimes are curbed or eliminated to the barest level. it is easy to have the names of criminals in each blessed day at the comfort of your room provided all the security institutions share intelligence reports and the names in the stations are properly fed into the public centralized portal showing the information (personal profiles with the pictures and contacts0 of the arrested criminals by the nature of crimes committed. The institutions could be free from criminals that are unveiled and sent to the security agencies by all other institutions like schools, hospitals, ministries, departments, agencies of government. Individual heads of ethno-religion in collaboration with the security agencies could release the names and bio-data of the alleged criminals within their circles.

Generally, the communications and information ministry should use the statistics from the bureau of statistics to create platform to have all bio-data of all individuals, institutions, structures and facilities across the nation for plans. For instance, all the information from the National Population Commission (NPC). The number of houses, business institutions, social residents, industrial layouts and others that are connected to the grid could be of great value to have the actual amount of VATs payable to the coffers on monthly basis.

ECONOMIC FUNCTIONS

ICT has undoubtedly brought up many businesses that would have failed initially. With this technology, instant producers customer relation is established. Through the internet, **email marketing campaign** has been one of the marketing tools helping to guarantee sales for products and services today. With email marketing, a manufacturer can push out sales messages to a million people at once. As against the traditional marketing, the response is instant. The manufacturer is able to get feedback and sales requests in thousands before the day runs out.

Many businesses have adopted **digital marketing; this enables them to** reach out to millions at a relatively short interval of time. In short, all professional bodies and institutions rely so much on the sector to perform maximally.

For the writers and publishers, ICT has helped spread articles, books and publications to distances it would never have reached through traditional means. Researchers publish the outcome of their research in order to disseminate their findings to the target readers and users through e-magazines and internet. Reports sourced from internet showed that in the United States, about **55,000 scientific journals** publishing about **1.2 million articles** for users, **60,000 books**, about **100,000 research reports** are issued per annum. The major **function** of publishing materials is to **educate** and **inform** the public about the solutions to their problems and challenges. The e-books and e-services are sold all over the internet via digital marketing. This generates several millions of dollars to nations that have enforced the VAT laws to be earning as addition to the selling cost. If for instance, Nigeria enters VAT remitting pacts with the e-commerce firms abroad to charge 1 dollar as Nigeria's VAT on every 10 dollar worth item to Nigeria as export, and there is record of 1m books, 5m films with each at the rate of 10 dollar per each, the nation shall earn **6m dollar** or more as VAT. One can now imagine the amount a large consuming nation like Nigeria would be earning as its own portion of VATs from abroad. The information from the courier services, the customs, the ports and other point of entries shall help the nation to have the right amount of imports to the nation from those companies abroad for claiming the right remit to the coffers. Convert the amount into the local currency.

The internet has also given birth to e-tutors and e-messages. We have seen online chefs, online tutors and consultants, online caterers, online schools, online kitchen, online parenting, telecommuting, telemedicine and many more producing online products for the increasing online consumers and shoppers (buyers for users). This is what we termed as e-message from e-tutors. Apart from this, jobs like editing, graphics designing, customer service and agency are now done over the internet; some Nigerians work full time this way without having to wear special clothing to work.

Thanks to ICT, e-markets and e-markets has increased. In this age, a man can lie lazily on his bed, order for a new television set and home appliances and get it delivered to his door that same day. E-commerce has given rise to the likes of jumia, eBay, konga, amazon, alibaba and others. Thanks to the internet, customer reach has increased thereby increasing sales, productivity and income.

Another is assembly sector; a phone casing can be manufactured in India, the panel in Japan and the battery in Finland then assembled in china. This is made possible by the exchange of dimensions and specifications over the air and the real time communication of exactly where a good or product is on the globe) Nigeria has an environment where records unrecorded for centuries can be collected in a digital platform to drive **knowledge-based economy**. If Nigeria is able to release **30,000 books** in different formats- paperback, hard cover and e-book per quarter, each tertiary institution professor releasing **5,000** journals per quarter, **5,000** articles per quarter, and each is fetching the nation just **50 naira** as VAT, the amount realizable runs into billions in a year. Nation could generate billions as VAT from the tracked books sold in big stores within and outside. From the publications and publishing sector, many talented writers from Nigeria are publishing in foreign online publishing firms and this can be replicated with the improved service of the communications and information sectors in collaboration with the education sector and the educational institutions spread across the nations. The online publishers are releasing thousands of books under their **Print-On-demand publishing agreement** just as **video-on-demand** from the entertainment sector. If the nation monitors the sales of these, several billions could be generated from the sector. Alas, the nation is not earning its own share while the advanced nations are smiling to banks. Let us look at the wealth created by the US mathematically in rough estimation. If the government of United States charges **.30 dollar** over each download of e-books per month, and **50 million of e-books** are bought through portals in the nation from different licensed digital right sellers and distributors, then the nation is making **.30 x 50 m** as VAT (withholding tax inclusive) on e-book alone for the month totaling **15m US dollars** per month. One good thing about e-book is that it is a product for all nations and book is like food to the body. People, institutions like libraries must have new books in new editions for the users. The book market would continue to grow as reading culture improves. Studies show that everybody reads intentionally and unintentionally. Even those who find reading printed materials (books, newspapers and journals) as boring do not have a choice than to read every day indirectly on phone as short messages, articles, breaking news, solicited and unsolicited mails, on the social handle, advertisements and tweets. Books are being repackaged in **abridge versions** for readers who do not have the time and interest to read long lines. Studies show that subscribers of e-books are in several millions across the globe. It is not necessary to be published books that are in paperback and hardcover formats, but **e-materials** also include all films, songs and even skills promoted and sold through communications devices.

Thanks to **e-transactions**; where a buyer can pay a seller party securely as fast as reading a nursery rhythm, digital distributors, e-book sellers with their **portals**, the van delivery businesses, courier services and postal service stations are made to boom by the presence and proliferation of the internet. As aforesaid, this also applies to the **Video-On-Demand** (VOD) makers, promoters, sellers and all other stakeholders. When goods and services are displayed (advertised) online for several prospective millions who are online, shoppers across the worlds, the need for payment for choice goods is also done by the communications devices The effective and efficient communications sector has marketed, promoted and converted many local products into international ones harvesting in billions of hard currencies.

The financial and non-financial institutions, in Nigeria today, most banks are operating internet-based banking, online payment and receiving digital platforms. Good example is **Gtpay** and **globalpay** of Zenith bank adding value to e-commerce in the nation. There are firms that operate e-money, mobile money, visa, verve, remita, mastercard, mobile wallet as innovations from affiliate e-payment gateway platforms like voguepay, paystack among other firms with transaction in local and foreign currencies. Meetings are held at the comforts of the offices through internet-based conferencing and thereby reducing the costs of transportation and other risks attached to travelling. Clients and contractors could hold official meetings with the use of social media handles like the use of video calls on instagram and whatsapp among other platforms. By this, the customers have access to Electronic Payment System (EPS) via different **e-methods** of depositing cash, transferring, payment of bills and collecting their money with different e-tools or e-services provided by the banks through the advancements in communications technology sector; goods and services are paid for in different or choice currencies online and offline. Through the advancement and regulations with **right frameworks** in the communications sectors in the nations, one can say that internet has created multiples of jobs than what the convectional businesses can generate. The online business is generating more gross domestic products and gross national income (GNI) than what the latter could per annum. Today, we hear of online media and media entrepreneurs, online television and radio stations from different disciplines. **Digital advertisements** are growing faster as all categories of people and institutions are embracing the technological innovations thereby slowing down traditional advertisements. In fact, many business owners make their goods and services of quality and the best for the prospective buyers through internet by leveraging on the outreach of advanced digital advertising to reach millions with a little advertisement expense. If the sales of business improve, more money would be deposited at banks for other commercial activities like business expansion, business diversifications, development and growth of innovations among others. The **digital social media** is so digitally connected that no user of the **social media or entrepreneurs** can do without buying either data or credits to access the internet. Towards generating jobs locally, the local digital media entrepreneurs could favorably compete with platforms created by the ICT gurus. Such platforms include facebook, twitter, instagram, Google+ and whatsapp. Some are introduced through **free apps** while some collect certain stipend. The fan must part with certain credits or data in megabytes before this app can be explored. In the modern communications technology terrain, **Facebook** claimed to have over 800 million subscribers, twitter has hundreds of millions of accounts and followers and **YouTube** has millions in excess 204m of uploads per minute as at 2015. In short, several digital entrepreneurs have been created and daily created from the internet services. Many are known for special purposes in apps. The presence of the digital business has simply created bigger platform for advertising and selling of products and services. The wise among people and institutions operate both online and offline to traffic enough clients for the business to grow.

In conclusion, for the economic and social functions to be effective, there must be procurement of the inevitable inputs such as the call credits, bytes for mobile data and mobile broadband at choice rate, affordable costs spread on different tariff plans by the operators.

From taxation, millions of subscribers are supposed to paid taxes and levies showing that government should as a matter of urgency to **improve revenue and employment generation brace up** to generate revenues from VATS:

a) Sales of credits cards

b) Sales of data plans and subscriptions of subscribers to enjoy cable services and transmissions especially by wireless cable media stations like Multichoice owned DSTV and GoTv, Startimes, kwese et al

c) Other ways by which revenues can be legitimately generated from the sector are:

i) Through penalty-attract reforms where shortchanging licensees are fairly fined

ii) Through the collaboration with ministries such as education ministry to operate reading tablets on billboards across the nation's tertiary institutions as discussed in the latter part of this book and the operation of close circuit television (CCTV) and other security gadgets on the major highways in partnership with the Ministries of Defense and Interior

iii) Through the fines collected from erred public as shown under i-reporting of vices by the people with clear evidences

N.B. The above increasing number of subscribers shall determine how much a nation generates from the sector to the national treasury if properly tracked and managed especially with relevant customized apps.

POLITICAL AND ADMINISTRATIVE FUNCTIONS

The world of politics is advancing. It is easy for nationals of a nation living in diaspora to have information about a party's manifestoes, its candidates and decide to vote for candidates of their choice with the use of their phones. In international and national contests and administration, voting to pick the right candidates are done through e-voting. There are plans, by the incumbent chairman of Independent national Electoral Commission (INEC) in Nigeria to avoid disenfranchisement of eligible voters for the efforts being made for the people in the prison yards, detention facilities, internal displaced persons' camps, hospitals and distant places to vote without moving out to the city where there are polling booths. No nation intends to be left behind. In the last general election in Nigeria, smart voter card readers were used to vote by the eligible electorates. This reduced to barest minimum the rigging of the politicians as it prevents the use of cloned cards. The **e-card**, of the registered voters, is recognized by the card reader machine (CRM) and the fingers of the voters including the showing of the face of the voter. The software used to produce the machine and the card made it difficult for the political parties to fake the voting materials.

In addition, government institutions, particularly MDAs at all tiers, are using telecom such as **servicom** of the Nigerian Communications Commission (NCC) in Nigeria for message delivery and feedback from people and institutions. This platform would have served certain status of whistleblowers a right medium to report the corrupt activities of officers in all offices and the public places. Are they effective as anticipated? Do the target users use the facility? The answer is NO! It is high time the unemployed Nigerians used the facility for public to change in all its facets as a form earning huge sum of money monthly. Several sites are purposely built and launched for creating social, political and economic apostles. Governments create social media platform and website to announce to the public their giant strides in office or simply to promote their welfare programmes. With some tap on google, information needed are at the beck and call of the browser without travelling distance and risk lives before getting the needed information. Nations can imitate on the benefits of advanced ICT to become exporter of books, films, songs, research materials from the local people to make both wealth and lucrative jobs for the citizens. Government can stop migration of its people from going abroad for better living and employment if the benefits of the sector are optimally tapped. With effective service from the ISPs and telephony operations, multi-tasking may not be too difficult to handle. **ICT savvy person** can be searching for hundreds of information within the same number of hours on the connected system to the internet without much stress compare to travelling and begging for these to be achievable with the right search engine optimization (SEO). The major gain is getting the materials needed at almost free of charge! A visitor to café can pay as a little as **200 naira** to surf and get information from papers being sold for **2000 naira**. He would have vital information he is supposed to traverse the lands to get at his beck and call. In the cyber café, he has the opportunity to read and read all stuff he needed aside downloading aspects he would like to go over again at his leisure time or at best print them out with his hard-earned money. Through internet facilities and inputs, no message uploaded can get lost unless the owner retrieve or retract it for personal or security interest. Versatility and creativity from natural intelligence in the use of computer could make retrieval of 'lost documents' to be as easy as a, b c. The security agents especially those tracking the **tax evaders** would use the search to unravel the evaders online without creating suspicions which may alert them to remove the vital information from the cyber space.

In retrospect, communication medium can be used in different ways to correct institutional ills and project the nation as a developed one in the comity of nations. Through **e-participation,** with influx of cheap mobile phones in the national discuss, many ills shall be corrected without wasting public funds. Does a nation need a convergent assembly of legislators when video-conferencing can do the magic? What about the institutions and businesses too? Since individuals communicate with ease with one another likewise public and private businesses and institutions can do with little funds, save of space and spare time is used for other profitable purposes.

E-money is in the economy through the advancement in the sector under new mobile money services. A lot of jobs were created for mobile money agents at different locations because of this. Point Of Sales payment (POS) system at shopping malls, fuel stations, hospitals and business outlets, the use of automated teller machine (ATM) to pay and deposit cash is an innovation that helps the financial sector to move with the global practice. People and businesses are now running cashless economy to safeguard the risk in carrying huge amount of cash around.

Security business has received a great boost by the communications devices. A time is near when electoral institutions would adopt **e-voting system** (EVS) to reduce costs and protect the electorates and the candidates. E-voting can eliminate huge investments in electoral processes and douse tensions in the nation. **E-campaign** would put effective end to hooliganism and destruction of lives and property during electioneering campaigns. **E-governance** would take governance to the grass roots with little funds. It is easy for people at the comforts of their homes, car-shops, offices, at parks, fuel stations, malls and all places to meaningfully contribute to the nation via working communication sector. Practicable solutions to national issues could be forwarded to the right authority with the adoption of the technology. It will be easy to send suggestions on what government can do to tackle the nation's crisis through e-governance. It will be easy to contribute to the discussions on the floors of the national assembly.

The breaking down of monopolies of the firms under the electricity generation, transmission and distribution would solve the problem of epileptic power supply in the nation. The elimination of monopolies of critical sectors may liberalize the sectors and the people and the nation is better for it. Many who are not part of the socio-economic think-tanks could have better ways to run the economy successfully. Many who are not politicians may have better path to tread to pave the way out of political logjams. Through special units adding their contribution to the cries of the stakeholders, those who are in charge would respond. It does not take a rocket science to know that voices have power (as in high volumes of decibels) and not a lone ranger voice which may be ignored as a mere child play. Using an anecdote, if only one person among large number who sees a thief raises alert, the voice may have been easily suppressed by the voices of others' non-challant attitude. But, if the large number of people shouted on the thief, it would attract more helping hands for nemesis to catch up with the thief. Information ministry can be effective with the deep involvement of the **communications institutions** and electronic devices under the supervision of the communications ministry. Conclusively, communications could be used to disseminate either positive or negative messages.

N.B. For all the **functions** to be effective by all the stakeholders, providers and the users, operating in the environment, there must be huge investments on all the infrastructures (manpower and equipment) by the private and public investors (government and regulatory agencies), and the purchases (increasing demands) of inevitable inputs such as the mobile data and mobile broadband at choice rate and tariff plan to run all the communications devices on the electronic platforms in particular.

HOW EFFECTIVE COMMUNICATIONS AND INFORMATION CAN RAISE THE NATION FROM DEVELOPING NATION INTO A DEVELOPED NATION

Having seeing the major users of the products and services of the licensees in the sector, certain inevitable steps must be taken by a third world nation to move up to become a developed nation in the ICT industry. We see this in two perspectives in terms of **employment generation** and **wealth creation and distribution**.

Firstly, communications ministry is responsible to reach out to the nation, people and institutions with processed collated information sourced from all ministries and agencies and regulating the sector for the overall benefits in wealth creation, technological advancement and employment generations for millions directly and indirectly through creation and management of a centralized portal where all activities of all MDAs are synergized through daily **reportage**. People, business and institutes can use the medium provided by the communication ministry to promote their business of the day. This can be done through necessary reforms for all the stakeholders towards achieving the set objectives (moving up the ladder). The reforms would assist the sector to track all **evaders of taxes** meant for infrastructural and social developments.

Secondly, it is a step to creating avenues for full employment of the idle hands (especially virile youths) that are in millions in the sector. Through the **reforms** as contained in the later part of this book, lucrative direct and indirect jobs would be created. Aside this, there are several ways to employ idle ones in the nation for a good cash rewards and national recognitions. The idle youths should be communicated to report what you witnessed as **ear witnesses** or what they witnesses as **eye witnesses.** This would fetch them some cash from the ministry.

If all vices are reported by Nigerians with cash rewards as the carrot, no one would dare involve in vices at any spot in the nation. NCC's **Servicom** in all public offices, schools and institutions are the avenues created to reach out to the government which is not optimally utilized. Let us use a recent crisis bedeviling the nation. There was a persistent fuel crisis recently across the length and breadth of the country. This has become a recurring issue in the nation especially towards the end of every year. Studies show that sellers hoard available fuel stock in their tanks and depots to sell at abnormal prices at nocturnal hours to favoured set of buyers. The hardship on the people and business could be imagined in a nation that is a crude-oil producing nation. Not only this, the threats to lives and property by criminals and terrorists are given the citizens insomnia. The **cyber-crimes** are on as hackers use **malware** to retrieve vital information and data of the original owners to infiltrate and intrude into the accounts. The adulterators and pirates are doing their illicit jobs to shortchange the nation and the genuine owners of works.

In fact, this has sent many 'lucky ones' out of jobs as unlucky ones have been sent to the world beyond. Most of the vices are common in the third world where the culprits go scot-free since the nation fails to maximally explore the potentials in communications sector. Many departments and agencies including the institutions are running at a loss due to bad communications or poor leadership in the management of the communications ministry.

Simply, truth be told, vices are too numerous in a land where communications is totally bad. All the vices can be nipped in the bud and thereby save the nation of huge sums of money for curbing crimes. Turning in the rate of crimes to a manageable size in the nation by all would turn the nation into a model nation for the rest. United States of America (USA) is able to get all data about crimes through certain organs of government showing the working institutions. Nigeria does not need to wait for the departments or agencies in charge of a piece of information to work on it. The customer care department of the electricity distribution should not be the only section to collect and collate problems of customers. Customers could send their messages through the Nigerian Electricity Regulatory Commission (NERC) or through a special unit in the communication ministry. The team of vigilance task forces on pipelines should not be the sole reporters of the act of vandalism. It should be a general task of everyone very close as witnesses to the data and news on how to nip the ill in the bud. We can all be the whistleblower as **agents of change** in the nation. We can all stop corrupt policemen on the highways if we can capture their pictures while extorting the road users of illicit money with the details and verifiable data. <u>This is not done for free but for a monetary reward</u> to motivate people and anti-corruption drivers to work with integrity. It should not be seen as duplicating services but as a complement to the works of those carrying the responsibility by act of establishing them.

What does the communications ministry need to do as complementary efforts? How would the ministry be making revenue for the government from this even though it has intended to 'employ' Nigerians to join in **reportage** <u>without incurring costs</u> of establishment at this austere time when the nation has being almost milked dry by the past administrations? Let the supervisory honourable Minister of the communications ministry take these steps:

First, create a centralize office (by conversion) at the state offices where all information and data are collected and analyzed for immediate use of the relevant owners to be managed by trained staff members or contracted expertise professionals. Equip the office with modern versatile **portal** that would feed the ministries, agencies, institutions of the government where information collected and analyzed are distributed to the genuine owners for prompt actions. The works of the staff members of the unit is to receive data and information from the people, institutions, associations et al from the public acting as the 'reporters' of events as eye witnesses and ear witnesses to the events that are threats to the nation and its citizens' socio-economic, political, technological lives.

Second, open and launch a website with portal that would be connected with all other ministries especially the information ministry where all collected data and voice information can also be properly disseminated to users daily. The site must contain senders' details including the names, address, the phone numbers, the email address, the picture if available and the content of the messages and the attachments as uploaded.. Verifiable data shall be treated as monetary rewarding content. Let us cite an example of verifiable data that would attract monetary reward. Such should give clear directive to the place of incident for those to take it up from there to arrive at the right time without wasting time roaming the streets. If for instance, there is a fire incident at 13, Rufai crescent, Leventis area Ibadan, Oyo state; the sender must, with some of the graphic details, give how the firefighters, policemen, and relevant agencies could get to the place by alternative roads within and around the ambience from different direction in a simple concise manner. <u>If the sender does not meet the requirements as concisely spelt out in the wall of the site, then such message may not be given official attention and does not qualify to earn cash rewards</u>. In addition, the site being managed by the staff of the communications ministry is meant for the collection of all forms of vices from the **i-reporters** wherever they may reside. Recently, I read that the megawatt of electricity generated by the transmission company has gone up to 4883MW from around 4,000 MW (The nation: Nov; 24, 2015) and confirmed by a popular radio presenter, activist and public commentator, **Edmund Obilo** then of Splash FM station programme of 'Voices' of <u>Saturday 28th of November, 2015</u> when he claimed that over 5,000 MW was generated as at the moment and the state was still in darkness Some of the vital media organs of government must disseminate the message to the public hence the public would be aware of where the fault of blackout lies. Later findings showed that it was the distribution companies that were not picking the generated megawatts to be distributed to the consumers of electricity. Watch the media stations and flood of messages of complaint flood the air. Complaints in one form or the others through calls, letters, mails and public speeches are always in the air. People desire to relay secrets of the evil doers and the saboteurs but they need right platform to be heard.

Generally speaking, people, businesses, institutions, streets no matter the location, the size, the status, affiliations, faiths and ideologies et al have rights to complain over any disservice, wrongdoing done to them, just to have quick redress. <u>This is enough to create jobs for millions of unemployed citizens</u> and get rewarded by cash accordingly as the reports would also increase the source of revenues to the nation's coffers. It is onus on the communications ministry in collaboration with the information ministry and relevant departments and agencies to politely create offices or revitalize NCC's **servicom** that would shoulder the responsibility to collect, collate and disperse the verifiable information and data to the right authority to act fast or be effective and efficient within the standard time. This activity is beyond the public complaints commission or the customer cares of the institutions. This is what we termed 'reforms' which appropriately suit the **change mantra** of the ruling party under the able leadership of **President Muhammadu Buhari** (GCFR). <u>Reporting vices is a national contribution to the growth and development of the nation</u> that is involving all Nigerians without exemption- the idle youths, the bloggers, the internet service business dependents, and all institutions to ensure smooth operation and growing Nigeria from a third world to the dream first world.

If a message of national importance and value is gotten from a local government area, such should be dispersed to the closest institutions that must come to the spot for redress. The reporters should be rewarded with **cash** for sending all the needed **facts and figures** with pictures to the ministry and motivated in several other ways as in awards, recognitions, to put all- people, institutions, businesses to tasks of reporting all what they see and hear in the public to the government. They report all the ills of the society directly to the ministry instead of sending the message to the security agencies that may not do the work promptly. Through the communications ministry acting as the government-owned **whistleblower**, all fuel stations hoarding fuel, selling above pump prices, calibrating fuel pump machines and meters, pipeline vandalisation, diversion of petroleum products away from the fuel stations to elsewhere, extortion of the public by collecting extra charges before dispensing the products, refusal to sell at certain time especially within working hours when the pumps are not down or the fuel attendants are absent at work among other nefarious activities in the petroleum sector just to swindle the buyers would be timely unveiled and communicated to the communication ministry's special monitoring unit serving as whistleblower to all other ministries and agencies; and the right ministry or agency would be informed to take the right actions at the right time. To safeguard the hours lost to queue for petroleum products, if the reporters unveil the name of the station, the place of business location, the time of reporting, the offences being committed among other **hard facts and figures** needed for the Department of Petroleum Resources (DPR), the security agents and the likes to work upon.

Third, make quick investigations through phone calls, text messages and mails to the right places and trusted people or institutions very close to the place to confirm the truths. Connect the law enforcement agencies very near to the place. The feedbacks from the agency would serve the unit to take the next step.

Fourth, transfer the critically analyzed data and information from the reporters to the right owners to treat promptly with the feedback from the security findings after the events have been reported at your portal. Sensitive matters that are of threat to the security and sovereignty of the nation should be done from the headquarters and undersigned by the right authority for further investigations and right steps to take.

As regards those information from human angle that are outside security threats which prompt action is needed, the information and data that should be released immediately to owners whose responsibility is to work on it to safe the nation and the nationals to prevent the ripple effects on the nation and nationals. This is from the special unit of the communication ministry shall pave the way for staff effectiveness and efficiency of the ministries, agencies, institutions and the most probable ill is nipped in the bud. This attitude is the actual **change** being anticipated by the people in the nation! This act serves a worthy reform to reform all the ministries and agencies. Before we say Jack Robinson, everyone, every institution, every agency, every department and ministry wakes up from their deep slumber and work for their earnings!

GENERAL GAINS TO THE NATION, THE PEOPLE AND THE MINISTRY

a) The cost of governance is tremendously reduced as the needed information and data that are reliable to work with are given out to the ministry to communicate to the right owners to give the best attention at the right time

b) The actual number of taxable items, individuals and institutions, within and outside the shores, are known to the nation. The amount of importing goods that are charged with VATs and the others are aware to the authority. And they could be active apps that would capture the payment without involving of the graft in any form especially in the diversion of the revenues to the private accounts.

c) More people especially the unemployed youths would be internet savvy within a short space of time. Those who do not know how to operate computer, surf internet, collate data and engage in technological services would learn and master the art.

d) It enables general participation in governance since it is a way of <u>reporting the reporters</u>, <u>watching the watchers</u> and getting involve and having deep interests in investigative journalism indirectly in order to unveil social malaise, saboteurs, infringements on rights and all other information needed for urgent attention.

e) Genuine Value Added Services (VAS) providers in collaboration with mobile networks operators would be unveiled for public prosecution and appropriately penalized and all sorts of illegally operating via unsolicited messages, unsubscribed automatic renewals of certain services especially on data plans, unsubscribed for caller tunes, illegal credit depletion and deductions without prior notifications among others would be a thing of the past. People, businesses and institutions who earned monetary rewards and recognitions (awards) for making available the sensitive reportage would see this act as a way of employing themselves. In fact, many youths that are unemployed but with the communication devices would see it as a way of indirectly employing them. One can imagine if a youth sends **10(ten) reports daily** on security threats being planned at different spots at different times with reliable empirical evidences as demanded in the site mailbox with all other required facts to the ministry and the authority in charge is briefed early to halt the evil action and such is paid a minimum of **one thousand naira** per good report meant for correcting a simple vice and ten thousand naira for greater vices. Such greater vices include alerting the communications ministry of pipeline vandalization, transformer vandalization, examination malpractice, armed robbery attack on bank, highway robbery. All these forms of reports would promote high moral values and integrity of the nationals. As regards, the monetary rewards to urge the reporters **into higher per**formance; for someone who is reported to report ten genuine cases, he or she should be earning a whopping sum of **one hundred thousand naira per day**! Such cannot use more than **five thousand naira** to buy credits to enjoy certain free megabytes to capture the pictures, get the message through voice records and forward the materials with his or her bio-data (with full addresses- email, phone contact, residential address, next of kin, account number) to the ministry at the state of residence. The estimates give a round figure of **several thousands of naira per month** and his/her total **expenses**(transportation, credits for browsing, depreciation of the phone, refreshments) could not be more than **fifty thousand naira** for the same period! This amount is more than what his fellows working in banks could earn per month! On the more technical reports and sensitive ones, a minimum sum of **above 10,000 naira** and above could be the agreed remuneration for the reporters per verifiable report. Such reports such as environmental pollutions like oil spillage, acts of terrorisms, financial crimes among others. If it is land pollution with garbage, such may not earn more than **10,000 naira** per reports as penalty for such may not be the same like pipeline vandalization, electricity equipment vandalization among others.

N.B. For all the functions to be effective by all the stakeholders operating, there must be purchases of inputs such as the mobile data and mobile broadband at choice rate and tariff plan.

f) Require more intelligence gathering before making reports from them. In fact, such could earn the reporter state recognition and huge cash sum.
g) In short, it is a good way to take the idlers among the employable youths even the unemployable out of the streets. In short, it will <u>create millions of indirect jobs</u> for the unemployed especially those dealing with digital products like mobile apps makers, digital sellers licensed by relevant department in the ministry and the retailers
h) The nation would be attractive to the local and foreign investors for its zero-tolerance to evil deeds. And the effectiveness and efficiency of the ministry to alert the rest would bring government dividends of democracy to the doors of the people with no stress. Through the adoption of **e-governance**, all ministries, departments and agencies of government can be assessed in a portal of the communications ministry.
i) The gross domestic products and the gross national income would be higher as all the bottlenecks have been removed or almost eliminated by the acting on the reportage
j) The staff in the ministry, <u>at the state level</u>, would be trained to handle the collection, collation and dispersal of analyzed data in summary form to the users at the state level. It does not need procurement of new staff except in a few instances where more technical hands are inevitably needed to complement the works of the existing staff. Collecting such vital information is not a duplication of duties. All hands must be on deck to sanitize the nation. It is a form of keeping all agencies to their toes.
k) Through the monitoring of the market situations with facts and figures, reporters from different marketplaces in the nation would help the ministry of finance, economic planning and budget to know how and what to do to run a booming economy. They would also be aware of the pirates, adulterators, smugglers of contraband, the fraudulent black markets, the bureau de change that extort the public, the banks that are working according to the ethics of the profession, the misappropriation of public funds among other illicit corrupt acts of the people and the public officers and institutions. There is no participant or active stakeholder in the economy would not think twice if they are aware of the **whistleblowers**

that would report them as independent i-reporters to the government's MDAs.
l) All causes of slow bureaucracy, bottlenecks, moral corruption, economic crimes would be eliminated in private and public service and the nation becomes the greatest beneficiary from effective and efficient service delivery
m) The nation would become a role model for other nations who do not know the effective way to curb crimes in all facets of life if the message is treated with utmost respect to restore sanity to all arms of government. In this case, there is no office, person or business too big to be reported. It is a situation where everyone watches his back. Everyone would be the first critic of self. Every business would check its performances. Every office lives up to require standard. Every organ of government would be up to task without all forms of crimes and criminality. And cooperation and coordination could be nearly perfect situation at all times.
n) Lastly, the communication having living up to its name would serve as checks and balances for all the ministries, departments and agencies and also become a cash-cow for the nation to generate revenues and creating jobs for millions. At this era of 'change mantra', the significance for the ministry to establish special units at all the state ministry to coordinate all others towards the developing the nation in all spheres of lives is a right peg at the right hole or round peg on the round hole as the maxim says.

CRITICS OF THE REPORTAGE FOR A PRICE AND PRIZE

There would be criticism over the reward of the reporters being indirectly employed by the ministry as regard where the money to be paid for the reports would come from. Another fear is the reporting of events with bias and sentiments. The fear of being attacked by those they reported might another factor that may delimit the activities and lastly, many feel that reporting is duplicating of activities of the other agencies under the law.

RESPONSES TO THE CRITICISMS

Through the power of legislation of the activities in collaboration with the ministry and the regulatory agencies (National Communications Authority (NCA) and Nigerian Communications Commission (NCC), each report would earn from the fines that must be paid by the offenders. A person arrested for adulteration of products through fine of **100,000 naira** as minimum penalty as most probably enshrined in the act establishing zero tolerance to adulterations; the communications ministry shall collect at least **25%** of the sum to offset the bills (salaries of staff working in each of the facilities across the federation) out of which the token of one thousand naira is paid the reporter. In the era of Single Treasury Account (TSA), all the money except the reporter's money is deposited at the treasury. One thing with crime is that crimes are committed every minute across the nook and corners of the nation but they are unreported or under reported not to talk of acting to stop the menace from spread through imitation. The nation would condone all crimes through the prompt reports acting upon and quick judicial process takes place. In short, it is a good way to make money every day to the treasury.

On the second criticism, in a multi-ethnic and multi-faith nation, it is expected to have elements of <u>bias and sentimental reportage</u>. This is where the analysts of the data and information in each state should analyze the reports critically before forwarding them to the right quarter for prompt action. The staff should be able to sieve the wheat from the chaff. The scam reports should be discarded from reasoning and some quick telecommuting to connect with the spots where a crime is being committed. Payment will be done after security agents within the jurisdiction have authenticated the confirmations. This effort would delay the reward for the reports to the next day or some days after the reportage.

On the third a reporter been attacked, all reporters have right to privacy of information reported. They would be protected by the **privacy and authenticity** of their bio-data. Secondly, reporters should learn how to investigate without creating suspicions. One can sit at the beer parlour in a state and records all the conversations of the bad elements drinking in the spot with his mobile phones, snap the arena from distance and gather all necessary information to alert the nation before the plotters hatch their evil deeds.

And lastly, all activities to ensure the nation grows and develops in all ramifications are not duplications but complements towards achieving the same objective. The security agents understand the need for sharing intelligence. This is the reason for the hiring of informants and establishing police community. Judiciary, legislatures, security agents (Police, Army, Navy, Air force, Department of State Security (DSS), Nigerian Security Civil Defense Corps (NSCDC), Nigerian Customs Service (NCS), Nigerian Prisons Service (NPS), National Drug Law Enforcement Agent (NDLEA), National Food and Drug Control (NAFDAC), Standard Organization of Nigeria (SON) need **reports** sharing to make them effective. This is called **intelligence sharing**. All their staff employed for the tasks could be effective without independent informants from the public. The communications ministry would only play a role of coordination and collation of the reports, analyze them, criticize them, and dispersing them to the owners for quick intervention.

WHISTLEBLOWERS EARNING FOR REPORTS REVISITED

Remunerated whistleblowers comprising the youths, the public workers, the bloggers, the social-media entrepreneurs, technology-savvy professionals and ICT-based institutes, the security agents among others are Nigerians who wish well for the fatherland. If there are one thousand people searching for news to be shared with the communications ministry each day on economy. All forms of **bad elements** and sharp practices in the market would soon become a thing of the past. On the fair side, any information or data sent that are fabrications after critical investigations and analyzes of the staff coordinating and collating them should attract certain **penalty** to curtail rumour mongers and false reports. This has to be communicated by the information ministry to the public through Ministry of Information and culture including its relevant agencies. Vices would keep evolving every day as not all can have adequate knowledge about **prescriptions and proscriptions**. Even the lawyers and the security agents violate the laws not to talk of the legislators!

All reports shall be generated from all offices, institutions, marketplaces and streets for the use of the stronger authority. If for instance, electricity distribution officials are collecting payments for bills from the customers by hand, this is a path to defraud the company. Such should be reported. If the traffic warders on the roads are collecting bribes from the road users, and such is captured in pictures and sent to the right site; the watchers have been watched and reported. When such offenders receive their punishment in forms of fines, the sanity would be restored on the roads. If a place where economic crimes and fraudsters are reported by eagle eyes people, such have their games up when they are arrested for prosecution. If the hoarders of goods in the market are caught red-handed and promptly reported no matter how highly placed such perpetrators are, the adverse effects on the prices of goods would be halted and the fines would add to the coffers of the government.

Meanwhile, the nature of the news, reports, abnormally, infringements, crimes, vices and all evils that are having negative effects on the nation's brand being collated and dispersed should be classified into strong or saboteur vices, weak and simple ones. Strong cases should be the highly penalized by the authority. How would revenues be generated to avert the recurrences of the vices being reported or to reduce them to the insignificant minimum? The table below shall be a guide per month per state as MINIMUM cases on average for **whistleblowing**:

TABLE I

VICES	FINE (N)	CASES	REVENUE GENERATED(N)
VANDAL(OIL facilities)	1 MILLION	100	100M
VANDAL(PHCN)	1 MILLION	200	200M
DIVERSION	1 MILLION	200	200M
HIKE PUMP PRICES	100,000	200	20M
FUEL PUMP calibration	100,000	200	20M
FUEL ADULTERATION	100,000	100	10M
SMUGGLING	1,000,000	1000	1BN
SOCIAL VICES			
ARMED ROBBERY	1,000,000	1000	1BN
ADULTERATION/PIRACY	100,000	20,000	2BN
LOOTING	100,000	100	10M
THUGGERY/CULTISM	100,000	10,000	1BN
ABUSES (DOMESTIC)	100,000	10,000	1BN
ENVIRONMENT (POLLUTION)	50,000	2,000	<u>100M</u>
			6.660 BILLION

The above estimates run into <u>over six billion naira per month</u> **per state** out of the **37-state** Nigeria. The estimates give **37 x 6.660** making **246.42 billion naira per month**. Heavier penalty can be placed on the treason and felony reported vices and others under criminal acts depending on the degree of sabotage on the economy and sovereignty status of the nation. And below are several cases that are not covered by the list.

The vices are too numerous to enumerate. **Vices** (such that fall under social, spiritual, economic, administrative, moral, financial, ethical and technological) come up every day in different dimensions and scale. Criminal engagements include kidnapping, burglary, raping, human trafficking, fake certifications, impersonation, drug trafficking, stealing by trick, financial crimes, sabotage efforts, treason and felony occur on a yearly basis with variation in number each year.

If all vices are reported to the ministry and fines are placed on each. If a **minimum penalty of 10,000 naira** is placed on <u>commonplace cases</u> of traffic offenders of all such including illegal parking and obstructions; in a month, a state cannot generate less than 2 billion naira from all the trunks of roads. If a public servant is found wanting as in lateness to work, demanding for inducements before carrying out a task being earned salary for is reported and such gets a fine of **5,000** naira, not less than **1 billion naira** would be realized per month as fine per state at outset. Indiscipline, moral and financial corruption would be eliminated in the public sector. The nation would generate <u>billions on monthly basis</u>. Has the reporting of cases not becoming a cash-cow to the nation?

Conclusively, a saying of the noblest among mankind was reported "<u>when you see an evil action, change it with your hand (scribble them down or stop it with your hands), speak against it (let the right authority be informed) …</u>" Therefore, all vices should be reported followed with hard and convincing fact and figures to sanitize all the institutions and places in the nation.

Report the shoddy jobs of contractors in the streets; **report** the kickbacks, bribery, and the likes at the public and private offices; **report** the malpractice and sharp practices at campuses; **report** all forms of saboteurs and piracy; **report** all lateness and moral corruption in all offices, institutions; **report** all social miscreants and nuisance; **report** all dark spots; **report** deserters at duties; **report** price manipulation at markets; **report** financial manipulation from banks; **report** all forms of illegality against the norms and values; **report** misconduct and unethical conducts of the professional bodies; check the excesses of the associations through **non-delayed reporting** etc

However, for this to work, **every report** must be free from bias and sentiments against faiths, ethnic et al. They should be truthful, reliable and transparent with no trace of sentiments. The first comprehensive or concise reporter of the same news is entitled to the cash rewards but all the reporters must be given due recognition via commendable letters as acknowledgements from the managers of the units at state levels.

And the fines from all the vices would be channeled as part of the revenues to the treasury for greater development. One can imagine the fines from **100,000 reported cases** of light vices per state per month whose minimum fine is put at **10,000 naira**. The nation has made a whopping sum of **37,000,000,000.00 naira** only (**37 billion naira only per month**!) Add this sum to the amount generated for the strong vices in the earlier table, the total money generated is (**37 + 246.42**) billion=**283.42 billion naira per month**.

PART TWO

COMMUNICATIONS AND INFORMATION SECTOR: NIGERIA'S HISTORY

In the previous administrations, it used to be information, communications and technology (ICT). It is established by the **Act** of national assembly particularly **Section Three of 2003 act.** Today, the change of name to communications ministry does not limit its function as the ministry supervising the telecoms and information sectors and the likes. All the communications and information mediums owned by the public and the private are under the supervision of the ministry. In the recent, there is proliferation of broadcasting media in the nation impacting in advertisements and public relation jobs. When the seat of power speaks, there is need for the communications and information ministry to be at the right track to get the messages properly and effectively disseminated. There is no business of government and individuals would not succeed without the inputs of the ministry. To achieve this, licenses are issued to private operators by the powers bestow on Nigerian Communications Commission (NCC) after privatization process of the ministry to achieve a reliable broadband plan at affordable cost of communications for the nationals and others. The entrance (license) of the **Global System of Mobile** networks (GSM) otherwise called **Mobile Networks Operators** (MNOs). Some of the licensed GSM operators under Communications Technology are MTN, Econet, Globacom, Reltel, Starcoom, O'net, Multilinks, Telkom, MTS, Visafone et al. Today, the FOUR popular mobile operators are Airtel (formerly Econet, Vodacom, Zain, Celtel), MTN, Globacom (Glo), Etisalat now 9mobile. In Ibadan, the capital city of Oyo state alone has about twenty radio stations running livestreaming broadcast, five television stations, three popular newspapers also running on social media handles, and several outdoor advertising companies among others that cannot do without the use of data and innovations from the communications sector. One can see the synergy of the two sectors in the nation building. And these have turned the communications and information businesses into a high pace in the procurement of data services and call credits at different tariffs and broadband plans. NCC introduced the portability into the sector for the subscribers' independence to switch from a network to another that can give better service under the Mobile Number Portability (MNP).

Before **liberalization of this sector**, only the Nigerian telecommunications (NITEL) was doing the telecommunicating job of <u>transferring messages</u> as a link from speakers to the decoders or receiver with the analog devices while Nigerian Postal Service (NIPOST) was solely in care of letter and parcel delivery to owners within and across the shores for a charge. Customers had no choice then just like the beggars. **Digital revolution** in communications sector broke the chains of the public companies' monopolies, with the licenses issued by **Obasanjo regime** to the MNOs. This utility that many neighbouring nations were enjoying in communications services was also birthed in Nigeria, the biggest African economy. In terms of internet-based market, in the African continent, Nigeria has over 107% penetration rate according to Buddie.com and 70% penetration of 168 million subscribers according to the Nigerian Communications Commission (NCC). The introduction and huge investments in the **evolution of broadband** for internet service providers (ISPs) became the revolution needed to boost the banking and educational institutions' efficiency and effectiveness. Also, research stations saved millions from travelling distance to procure data for their works.

Today, educational institutions are using **e-libraries. E-learning, e-tutorial** and online research stations for **e-students** and **e-tutors** using **e-books** and **e-materials** are being embraced by institutions especially for the part-time and correspondence students living far away from the schools. The students also use e-payment to make payments for purchases like books and kits and all fees payments. Computer based tests (CBTs) are fast replacing the conventional mode of conducting tests. Thousands of call centres, cyber cafes sprang up across the nation. This also paved the way for bloggers to proliferate. The cost of transportation, medical expenses from the stress of travelling and other gains have been grossly reduced by the cheap and affordable communications devices in the booming interconnectivity and intra-connectivity sector in the ministries.

By mathematical illustration, the Subscriber Identity Module (SIM) cards, to store both credits and data keep increasing to over one hundred million in the nation. Over one hundred million Nigerians are customers purchasing airtime, mobile data and broadband services by the licensees. In fact, the Wikipedia search on internet confirms that **70%** of **over 168 million**(around 117 million) are users of SIM cards(mobile) as at **third quarter of 2013** though NCC website page puts it at over **148 million** as at the 3rd quarter of the year 2015. The subscribers to CDMA provided by Vodafone and Multilinks Telkom are around two million at the same period.

The users of SIM cards vary from students of secondary school to those at the tertiary institutions to big entrepreneurs and firms. Some of the customers have at least **two SIM cards** of different networks and others for **apps** like whatsapp blackberry, customized androids and not less than eight out of ten browse daily with either their phones, desktop, laptops or on different brands of **tablets**. For internet activities on these **smartphones**, monthly subscriptions are paid for data as prepaid or post-paid for either retail or bulk subscribers. The bargaining on the transaction is based on the classes of buyers or subscribers. Licensees desire to sell in large volumes with token gain if bulk buyers are available in order to save certain costs.

With the influx of cheap fairly used smartphones by importers, networks providers started giving out free data to attract most customers possible to their networks. The free megabytes serve as a gift of data after making a prescribed recharge. Some networks dole out free 10MB for 100 naira card purchased valid for seven days, 'terms and conditions' apply. Users with much heavy internet dependence have to recharge more buy more megabytes or gigabytes of data as needs demand. Most subscribers browse for e-materials, e-news, uploading and downloading of free e-books, songs and films at no additional deductions from their airtime balance. Several millions can read newspapers globally on mobile phones more than before. Transferring of files is easily done with the data on every credit purchased for calls. Many can transfer money on air with the data on their phones. These huge benefits is a confirmation that the number of subscribers would keep growing per day.

This number of users outnumbers the total number of population of seven sub-tropical African nations. To the operators, Nigerian market is the market to explore profitably. It is a nation whose people have love for good things that create essentials of lives at any cost.

COMPETITION IN THE MARKET BY OPERATORS

At the outset in Nigeria, calls were charged per minute until the advent of the third-licensed MNO, **Globacom** owned by the billionaire entrepreneur, **Mike Adenuga**, who introduced **per second billing** (PSB) for calls. The craze and crave of subscribers to <u>per second billing</u> by subscribers turned the table for the sector as others also introduced boosts to be relevant in the sector. At this period, there was no free short message service, no free night calls and no off-peak prices in the charges as all times are peak periods, no free data services for browsers.

The internet cafes charged exorbitant browsing fees as much as **500 naira per hour** per user on users depending on the place of business locations. At the point, the network was generating income from selling both credits for private rich subscribers and boosters for call operators where the network covered. International calls were too high in cost for callers. All services from the MNOs are expensive; only a few institutions and rich individuals that could afford the costs. Market penetration was low. Those who could afford to own a sim and a phone sometimes do not get recharge cards available at their reach. The sector, first by MTN, introduced virtual top-up (VTU) credits through their retail outlets and later from banks automated teller machines (ATMs). At the moment, a subscriber need not go outside his room as he can purchase airtime over the air by paying with his bank account.

INTERNET SERVICES AND SERVICE INSTITUTIONS: GAINS AND DRAW-BACKS

Today, credits are not just bought, they are shared from subscriber to subscriber and also borrowed from network providers through auto borrowing/sharing among several innovative ways as illustrated under **business function** of communications technology. The internet service providers provide CDMA services which make availability of data services to the users. Also, many online or virtual educational and business institutes have gone virtual. This new dimension in the sector apparently makes it difficult to track the volume of sales of credits and data.

School fees, electricity bills, cable subscriptions and other utility bills are paid online just like shopping and making payment online for all purchases. GPS (Global Positioning System) and map of projects are located through internet devices by surveyors and related professionals. Mapping is no more difficult with these devices when they are online. The sailors and pilots are more efficient than ever before. Tutors and researchers rely much on information from the search engines created by internet.

On the other side, government agencies are losing to the participators huge sum from **value added taxes** alone not to talk of **corporate sales tax** among others. This can be halted with the package of software where the code must be used at source by subscribers in order to get remittance instantly. Let us cite an illustration. If a network uses **x22xpin#** to load the credit or data purchased. There should be collaboration between the government regulatory agency (NCC) and the MNOs to have a universal loading code which will transfer dues to different accounts at the point of purchase. The code could look like this **x22x11xpin no#** where **22** is where the share of the company would go, the **11** is what is remitted to the government coffer from the amount loaded in form of the **pin no**. The hashtag (#) shows 'okay' or 'I agree'. Software should be produced for those who buy from automated teller machines to get the same result. To the financial strength of the nation, the huge billions per month directly from taxes would eliminate dependency on the revenues from the petroleum sector.

Other gains of the sector are too huge to elaborate in a few words especially in human capacity development. Walk the streets and you would not be surprised to see 'school-on-air'. Manpower is easily developed with the advent of communications industry. This is made feasible at the presence of internet services and mobile countryside telephony. The improvement on the reach of the MNOs through expansions paves the way for numerous phone brands entry into the nation from all ports and boundaries. It may be impossible to have the actual number of phones with Nigerians. The evolution in the phone industry keeps improving by the day. The nation has moved from analog to digital phones. We are now in the world of **androids, ipads, iphones, windows phone, tablets, laptops** and **palmtops** from different brands. *Unfortunately, consuming Nigerian market has not produced indigenous phone.*

Billions of Naira are injections from Nigeria to create wealth and lucrative jobs to the exporting nations. Talking more about the possibilities through the inception of the operators, one can vividly say that Nigerians are catching on to the advanced nations. Yet, many things we should have keyed into to transform the nation from 'importers' of everything to exporter of most things with the bounty of natural resources at our disposal. Nigeria is blessed with huge intellectual resources including writers, researchers, thespians, artistes, innovators, engineers, technologists and scientists whose work can generate millions of employment opportunities and thereby generating billions to the Gross Domestic products (GDPs) and Gross national Income (GNI).

Today, National Open University of Nigeria (NOUN) and convectional university Distance Learning Centres (DLCs) are run effectively with the use of internet services at cheap costs. It is without doubt that all businesses in the nation have mobile network operator supplying them what they need in mobile infrastructural services. Rural telephony is becoming a reality gradually with increase in the funding and expansion policy of the MNOs.

A major setback to improve every business and aspect of our lives with this sector is the **epileptic supply of electricity** to power the industries particularly the development of variants of sought-for software in the sector for the **e-solutions** being advocated for. Companies have to rely on the software from abroad to work with. We become importer of what we can also manufacture locally. Nigerians who have brains in software engineering and programming are lost to nations abroad under **education tourism** or search for jobs after training. This is a cash withdrawal, in foreign currency, from the economy and a major reason for the much-demands for dollar at the peril of **falling Nigerian naira** in the foreign exchange market not to talk of the parallel market. Manpower development for the sectors and for the proliferation of several businesses such as online media stations, online retailers and distributors, bloggers, online publishing, online bookshops, online libraries, electronic reading billboards among others are alien in the nation. This deprives several thousands of lucrative jobs.

On the part of the licensees and their subscribers, several millions are not properly registered. In the recent, data lost led to the ban of lines of subscribers. Many of them had to undergo stress and spare valuable time and energy again to re-register their SIM cards. This reduces the confidence they have on the MNOs and the consequence may have negative effects on the security of the nation.

Records from newspaper reports show the increase in the **cyber criminals** and **fraudsters** calls on phone networks. Unfortunately, the information about the fraudsters always remains secret with the MNOs until legal action takes place. All over the world, the users of ISPs are protected by certain laws that established the information and communications sector. Everyone, individual, institution, business and entity has right to have his message kept as secrets from the third party. But, if such illicit messages become a threat to the sanctity and human right to the extent of threatening the sovereignty of the nation as in the cases of terrorist groups, armed robbers, kidnappers, hackers, spies, pirates and all other criminal elements using the facilities (telephony and website data services) to meet and network, carrying out their nefarious acts, causing harms and loss of lives and property, then there is inevitable need of **reforms** in the sector.

In the field of studies, it is learnt that terrorist groups recruit via internet; vital information are passed through the medium; several attacks on places are coordinated through the phones and internet services; businesses secret reports are hacked into via the internet and software and the art of manufacturing explosive and dangerous devices are made available via internet. Gone are the days when the illicit acts are properly monitored, the difference and the conflicts of political ideologies and the emerging of allies has created loophole for all the bad eggs to operate with ease. Nations hardly share intelligence reports even if such is aware of the plan attacks on the cyber space of the disgruntled elements.

The MNOs claim to have problems with the Value Added Service and others who have rights to purchase data in bulk and retail use their platforms to dupe the subscribers of their credits in form of unsolicited packages and data plans. Many deduct through the short codes on the phones of the subscribers. This is another challenge for the communication ministry and particularly the Nigerian Communications Commission (NCC) to build new software developers for **e-solutions** to stop the criminality tendencies.

DEVELOPING SOFTWARE DEVELOPERS AND PROGRAMMERS BY AUTHORITY

There are steps to take:

a) Create enabling technological environment with the massive investment in the building of communications and information infrastructures with all the modern equipment and support of adequate and cheap power supply
b) Collaborate with all professional institutions producing software engineers and developers to produce competent graduates. The churning of quality human capital from the tertiary and specialized institutions shall make a big impact on the growth of the sectors.
c) Engage the graduates after their courses with attractive welfare packages
d) Research for what the businesses, institutions and individuals need in software which are to be given to the employed engineers to work upon. By this, foreign importation of software would be a thing of the past. There should be domiciled apps for all the sectors especially the electricity and the power, the transport, the communication, the security institutions, the information and the education sectors to enhance collection of revenues with electronics.
e) Emphases should be on how to develop loading codes with the licensees and other payers of VATs and other dues in order to assist the government to get the right taxes at source. It will eradicate tax evasion and generate billions each month for national uses.

f) Create software, by the ICT staff members that are specialized in the production, to track the register subscribers and the new ones in order to curb insecurity in the nation and its shores.

To get work done, there must be declaration of emergency in the communications sector by the legislative and the executive arms of government. Building of communications technology infrastructures require massive investment to have the latest equipment and professional experts.

HOW THE MNOs ATTRACT MORE SUBSCRIBERS EACH QUARTER

We have mentioned this a bit at the earlier pages. It is showing the versatility and dynamism of the marketing and sales department of the licensees. This is the use of marketing and selling strategies under the promotional campaigns that are legal in the face of the **NCC Act** that established the firms. Let us look at a few methods.

A network may advertise that buyer or subscriber who purchases **200 naira** worth of airtime would enjoy **800 naira airtime** to call all networks that would valid for a week with **'terms and conditions'** apply slogan. Many subscribers, especially the poor prepaid ones, who are used to managing 100 naira for a week before would be lured into buying 200 naira card. Secondly, since his reach is wider than before; such would be addicted into connecting to more people to talk with. Thirdly, the **chatting addiction** would have created habit of talking more than necessary unlike before and his rate of buying more credits become higher. **Studies**, from field reports, confirm that many below average (poor) subscribers- mostly the illiterate artisans, who used to spend **200 naira a week** are now buying more than **1000 naira in a week**. The **free credits** that are targeted at 'adding more values' to the caller would never last the valid date of the recharge before it vanished into a thin air.

In another dimension, many mobile subscribers have flair for sending photos, bulky messages and files online through the mobile phones. The **free data** in megabytes attached as free gifts from the MNOs is a **bait** for them to procure more credits than anticipated. Those who used to buy **four hundred naira call airtime** would be persuaded to buy **1000 naira per loading** to enjoy the free megabytes. Many who like to read newspapers instead of visiting the news vendors have to buy adequate credits to enjoy **free megabytes** to read. Many who are song lovers and film addict cannot do without downloading on their phones and laptops with the available bytes either purchased or gotten free from the credits purchased for calls. The activities of the VAS and the indirect imposition of unsubscribed **callertunes** subscriptions is another way the MNOs shortchange the customers of their credits. Only the literate may take drastic steps to recover their **lost credits** to questionable '**terms and conditions**' and discontinue the art of cheating. Many others withdraw their complaints after facing a dead wall.

SUGGESTED SOLUTIONS TO REGULATE THE VAS AND MNOs

We find it a conspiracy for the VAS to be using the facilities or the platforms of the MNOs to carry out the illegal extortion of the consumers' credits. The MNOs are like *bankers* for the subscribers whose sole responsibility is to manage the credits of the VAS subscribers. They must have a working portal that only deduct what the customers genuinely used in the services from the MNOs only. We suspect that the VAS is an arm of the MNOs for the fraudulent activity to be going on unabated. This menace of unsolicited Value Added Services (VAS) can be curbed with these steps by the legislature endorsement in collaboration with the other arms of government:

a) The MNOs must alert the subscribers of the message that emanate from them before they fall victims to the illegal VAS
b) All recognized VAS by the MNOs must be unveiled and communicated to the subscribers via adverts first

c) MNOs. Should track the all third party VAS on their portal and should track the **short code** to the account of the senders (VAS)
d) The MNOs must develop a software to expunge the unknown VAS from the first day
e) The NCC must create portal to track the possible sales of the VAS and by so doing the value added taxes could be calculated and claimed from the MNOs.
f) All the strange VAS must be outlawed and punitive measures taken against them to prevent others from joining the bandwagon.

ASSETS AND LIABILITIES OF THE MINISTRY

These are what it inherited from the previous ministries where it emerged. They include:

a) Nigerian Telecommunication (NITEL)
b) Nigerian Postal Service (NIPOST)

NITEL has its facilities (stations and masts) across the six regions of the nation. It was operating analog with six digits with each state having its three digit dialing code.. NIPOST stands for Nigerian Post with post offices and letter boxes in all capitals, big towns and states of the federation.. The former attended to the speakers on phone while the latter was for the letter writers and parcels dispersal working in the stations and sub-offices across the nation. In all, both NITEL and NIPOST have stations, offices and infrastructures that are assets all over the federation. However, a lot of these assets have been out of service for a while some are obsolete; thereby turning some into liabilities. For the communication sector to run at optimum, **mobile infrastructures** are inevitable. This comprises the physical structures, masts, satellites, equipment, machineries and the logistic supports from the management of the ministry and its agencies.

EFFECTS OF PRIVATIZATION AND COMMERCIALIZATION OF THE COMPANIES

Through the Bureau of Public Enterprises (BPE) Act, communications sector was liberalized. Monopolies of the NITEL and NIPOST were broken to pave the way for the private investors since 2000-01. The public-owned companies were handed over to private owners to manage especially the Nigerian Telecommunications (NITEL) which resulted in the name change from NITEL to Mobile Telecommunications (MTEL). The private-owned mobile operators become active participants in the communications business sector.

By this privatization, there is multiple of abundance of information and data from internet service. Gone are the days when users of information and data found it hard to get anticipated volumes. Data, censored and non-censored, quality and not quality, reliable and not-reliable... flood the air every day. It takes the searchers of information and data to engage in further research studies and critical analyzes to pick the best reliable ones for use. Each of the participants in the communication sectors is having millions to serve thereby increasing the competition.

Intercoms services provided by the MNOs on an agreement with the management are at banks and schools for easy mobilization and coordination of administrative activities within the institutions. People who can afford it have intercoms connecting all rooms as we have in hotels, hospitality and security businesses. Government institutions and Non-Governmental Organizations (NGOs) also pay for intercom services to reduce cost of prepaid credits for their staff members within the offices and branches at the working hours. Through the liberalization of the sector, several online businesses have proliferated within a short time in the nation. Many online businesses have grown and e-commerce activities have taken over the nooks and corners of the nation especially in the southwestern Nigeria. Today, the likes of jumia.com, konga.com, kaymus.com, yudala.com and professionalized sites are on air. Although the facilities are not tapped to the fullest, Nigeria is moving up the ladder by economic prosperity and constant growth..

Many prosperous **Print On Demand** (POD) publishers rely more on the online services and the active participants in the online retailing and wholesaling to sell their books. Nations have ability and the legal rights to earn VAT over all the purchases and imports into the nation of books instead of declaring them duty-free. The locally-produced books should attract reduced VAT and other taxes and not the imported goods, films and others. Browsers of internet for information can google internet in search for self-publishers that are PODs.

Let me share my personal firsthand experience. I browsed internet for publishers of my unpublished materials some years ago. At a few a tap on the search engine, the likes of BBB-rated authorsolutions firms namely authorhouse, iuniverse and xlibris were found. In fact, the process of the POD from the study of the publishing packages showed that it is a kind of job that requires other people's money and other people's minds (OPMs) to start. It is simply **zero-capital business** (ref: Jobs with zero capital Vol. Two). The online companies are selling to countries all over the world with the use of the channels of distribution. All these transactions must add certain amount as VAT to the nations where the products are produced. What about the receiving or the consuming nations? Don't they have the rights to some VATs too of the imports to their nations as part of forex earning source to the coffers of the nations?

A difference in the privatization and commercialization is that as private owners of communication businesses are licensed and enjoy the available mobile infrastructures to operate, the public-owned become commercialized to make profits. This creates competition to beat down the prices for tariffs and charges.

With the gains from ISPs, all makers and promoters of intellectual materials and skills are opened to massive patronage. Today, the singers are amassing wealth from the huge adverts they have while their single hits attract millions of followers and thousands sometimes running into millions of downloads. Many radio and television stations are already reaping from online services. Some radio and television stations in the advanced nations make money from popularizing their stations with quality interviews and investigative journalistic works upload on air for viewers and listeners across the world. I have come across some of these in the course of selling and promoting my publishable materials.

IDEALS OF THE COMMUNICATIONS MINISTRY

From the studying of the contents of the regulatory agency, Nigerian Communications Commission (NCC), one can infer that the ministry has its unique **ideals** as enshrined in the mission statement of the ministry. Some of these ideals are summarized below in lines:

a) To create framework in practicable contents for the development and improvement on the mobile infrastructures for enhancement of effectiveness and efficiency of all institutions and people through the powers of the NCC.
b) To create enabling environment for private operators and public institutions work to better the communications level of all the stakeholders and users
c) To create avenues for the building of software to make proliferation of **e-commerce** possible and effectively halt **e-fraud** for all forms of products and services
d) Turning the ministry into a **cash-cow** from the licensing of operators of different categories like the advanced nations and creating mouth-watering earning jobs from the sector. Studies confirm that Information and Communications Technology (ICT) which paves the way for improving electronic world is the highest employer of labour and the cash-cow to most economies.
e) And set the nation free from the scourges of unemployment and underemployment facing the nation as a threat.
f) Signing technological partner in the transfer of information and communications technology with affiliated partners to train the nationals

and their technical agents within towards improving the human capacity and local content from the gains
g) Synergizing of the ministries through centralizing the functions of the ministries and agencies towards achieving e-governance and quality administration

REGULATORY INSTITUTION UNDER THE MINISTRY

A major regulatory body under the ministry is the Nigerian Communications Commission (NCC) whose headquarters is in Abuja. It has numbers of function such as:

a) Licensing of the telecoms operators under these classes like sellers and installers of terminal equipment for mobile cellular phones and HF/VHF/UHF radio etc; repairers of telecoms facilities, cabling service providers; cyber café and public payphone services under **class licenses.** The other licensees are those who have internet service, prepaid calling card, sellers and installers of satellites, GSM providers, electronic directory information services, fixed wireless access under **individual licenses**, among others like value added services providers.

b) Regulating the works of the association of licensed telecoms operators of Nigeria (ALTON) to safeguard the customers' privacy rights and ensure quality service with the amount paid by the subscribers. This also includes the inspections of their books of accounts; revocation of operating licenses among others.

Several are greater in the creation of imply jobs expected from the supervisory ministry over the activities and powers of the NCC. Some of them are:

a) Ensure that all subscribers identification mobile(SIM) cards are properly registered before use or become operational

b) Ensure that the registered cards owners have their proper records of identification with the office
c) Coordinating all the activities of the users and subscribers against the Nigerian state of economy, politics, technology et al in a way that they have values for their credits and gigabytes or megabytes
d) Ensure that all data of the licensees especially the cyber cafes, the professional institutes, the sellers and installers of the licensed firms are with the NCC for tracking on taxes and levies due to be paid to the coffers of the nation.
Studies confirm that many cyber cafes <u>do not</u> have certificates of registrations and also the same with the accredited and various forms of dealers in the assets of the MNOs such cards major distributors and marketers.
e) Ensure that the addresses of the subscribers are verified before such could use the SIM card for personal or business purpose in the centralized portal under the supervision of the ministry and its regulatory agency, NCC.
f) That all cards must have separate reasons of purchase for security reasons
g) That all networks operators enter into agreement of cooperation to release illicit messages by air (phoning, text messaging via short message service, bulk message service, blackberry message, posts et al) to their portal at request for security intelligence reports to the right quarters.
h) Ensure that all internet service providers are duly registered with all information about those guarantors for the firms in case of insecurity of lives and property
i) Ensure that it works with security intelligence and enforcement agents to track the illicit usage of the facilities
j) Compare notes with intelligence agencies time to time
k) Ensure that unregistered owners of SIM cards and internet services are blocked time to time to protect the lives and property especially the nation's integrity.
l) And lastly, there must be collaboration efforts between the operators and the major stakeholders selling all the credits and data to produce specialized **software** where the taxes are deducted from the source or

point of payment. This should work in a way that all subscribers, retail and wholesale among the prepaid and postpaid must get their VATs and other calculable taxes paid at source (payment point). A **code** of loading must be developed in a way that government would earn its due at the spot.

With all the above, security of the nation must not be compromised by any criminal elements under any disguise of religions, business, culture, ideology. These are part of the reforms to save billions being lost in goods and services to fraudsters and terrorists.

PROBLEMS OF THE LICENSED OPERATORS

The operators, from our field studies, face these challenges of disenabling business environment:

a) <u>Multiple taxations</u>: Most businesses in the nation complain over multiple taxations. The result of this is that if the companies do not close down because of this, the burden is passed on to the subscribers in form of hike in the costs of services. The mobile network owners charge different packages with different forms of tariff plans with hidden **terms and conditions**. Our studies show that many firms hide on frivolous 'multiple taxation' to evade taxes. This complaint is intentionally done to attract the sympathy of the public. And the price burden is directly passed unto them. If all the calculations done in this book are duly and **critically verified and tested** by authorities, the fact remains that most of the companies are not paying the actual taxes especially the VATs to the government coffers. Government can stop collecting other taxes to reduce the taxes being collected provided the companies agree to pay the VATs at source with e-payment or automated payment system without involving a person.

b) Epileptic supplies of energy particularly electricity supply: The ripple effects of epileptic supply of electricity and the huge cost of fuelling the generators on the business are becoming a threat to the survival of the business.
c) <u>Poor topography for mast erections</u>: Certain areas do not support erections of mast towards target reach of the firms. As a result the masts and other needed facilities may never be built or built at a cost way too high. In most cases, the operators are left with the option of building at an exorbitant price because if it is left undone, this would lead to poor services, intermittently loss of signals, dropping calls and loss of customers to competitors.
d) <u>Cultural challenges especially on the land holding system</u>: It has been a difficult issue to get right places for the erection of masts. Government does not invest much to assist the operators to get land resources with the use of land use decrees. It is therefore increasingly expensive for the operators investing hard-earned financial resources in the nation.
e) <u>Bad networks of roads</u>: The investment in the sector gulps billions of dollars especially to meet the global standard practice in the sector with the procurement new modern devices and equipment for their base stations and for fibre optic transmissions. <u>Short supply of capable manpower from poor form of graduates from tertiary institutions</u>: Most schools in the federation run a few relevant technical courses needed for the investments as most of them are not accredited to run the courses. The reason for non-accreditation of relevant courses is the deficiency of infrastructures and professionals to handle the courses. It is therefore costly to the business to procure their capable technical staff from abroad. Those recruited from abroad would be paid in foreign currencies and this adds to the costs of production.
f) <u>Poor attitude to intelligence sharing and slow bureaucratic processes</u>: Government agencies are run by lazy workers. These slow down the processes of the investors.
g) <u>The unregistered value added service</u>: Many have fallen victims of the Value Added Services (VAS) providers that are illegally using the platforms

to dupe the subscribers through illegal deductions of their credits for unsubscribed messages.

The identified problems have practicable solutions. Studies show that companies always hide under **multiple taxations** simply to **evade taxes**. Many publish paper profits to fulfill all righteousness with frivolous profit before tax (PBT) and profit after tax (PAT). Many shareholders who are stakeholders do not care to demand for the breakdown of the taxes. By this attempt, the actual sales from the value added tax would not be known. These taxes, being evaded include **value added tax** (comprising withholding tax), personal income taxes, corporate sales tax and some levies that are government dues. If the businesses pay at least the already charged and deducted at the point of sale; the VAT, the nation would be **generating hundreds of billions per month** to grow the system without borrowing. With the dues paid to the coffers, the dearth of social infrastructures needed would be solved with the available funds from the sector.

Nevertheless, the challenges of the operators are some of the problems facing the ministry to achieve set objectives at standard time. On these, **inevitable reforms** which we identify as broader reviews of the powers on NCC, the regulatory institution, must take place urgently.

EFFECTS OF UNREGISTERED SIM CARD AND ISPs TO THE NATIONAL INTEGRITY

The effects are negative to the nation and the institutions. Some of the ripple effects are:

a) Illicit transfer of cash from the original owners to fraudulent accounts of collaborators
b) Retrieving of sensitive and security data without legal permission

c) Infiltration into the information and data to alter evidences and exhibits. Many fakers of certificates of schools, businesses and vital documents sneak into archive to retract and doctor the data and information. Also, the destruction and adulteration of evidences may truncate judicial processes in courts of law, the flow of information towards smooth effective and efficient of a corporate institution, the funds movement between the financial houses and the stakeholders, the conclusion of election process et al

Nations, through the communications ministry or relevant agencies, must ensure all operators of mobile technology and their SIM cards, not excluding the ISPs, are properly registered for the following reasons:

a) To safeguard the use of the medium for nefarious criminal activities. Once the criminals or the intending criminals are aware that they are operating in the 'day', they may decide to turn a new leaf. For instance, those who hack lines and sites could develop software for the defence agency for security of the nation. Those who are into malware and virus creation may use it for better software that would grow the economy and technology.
b) To intercept or even cut the flow of information of the criminal elements. Many vices like kidnapping, financial crimes, burglary could be detected and unveiled through the registered and kept records of the users or clients. If certain unregistered lines are being used to carry out the criminal activities
c) To protect security information from spies and their agents. This is safety at the highest order. All owners of works (products and services, data and information) would be rest assured that their works are intact and safe.
d) To manage encrypted information and data for security reason
e) To network all databases of all institutions so as to enable them share intelligence on the cyber-crimes. It is easy for the nation to track crimes in any form from the registered databases with all records kept intact for immediate or future use. The issue of tax evasion may be a thing of the past with the database information and unhindered digital revolutions.

f) To remove fear from the minds of individuals and institutions in their separate activities. The assurance that a lost item (information, data, and personal resources like money) shall be recovered through the software and the database connectivity would eliminate all forms of fear from all (individuals, businesses, institutions) across the nation.

HOW TO PREVENT UNREGISTERED SIM CARDS AND INTERNET SERVICE PROVIDERS FROM CIRCULATION IN THE CYBER SPACE

Several **reforms** can be used to stop the menace. Some are:

a) Block the cards and the ISPs links with the use of adequately monitored portals
b) Employ licensed hackers to legally hack the data and sensitive information from such lines before it is pulled down for the owners to face prosecution. The criminal materials, sieve from the lines, are the exhibits for prosecution at the right time in order to get fair hearing at the court.
c) Software can be developed to attack such unregistered lines and links. Feed all the registered on to the portal and use the software to recognize the original and the properly registered ones while the unregistered ones are barred from making headway.

PART THREE

"Versatility and creativity is the tool
Urgently needed to turn the sector into cash-cow"

COMMUNICATIONS AND INFORMATION SECTOR, A CASH-COW; HOW?

Outside what the nation can generate as VATs, the fines, corporate sales taxes and from **tracking the sales** of call credits cards and data, there are other ways by which the nation can generate revenues for the nation. This would add to the dream status of the ministry- turning it into **cash-cow**. Communications is vital to our modern day survival, from electronic **mail** (popularly referred to as email or letter – on –air) to short message services, bulk message service, blackberry messengers, transfers, chat rooms, yahoo messengers, **internet calls,** digital tools like the video calls through **skype, whatsapp, instagram** et al to **speedy** courier services for the letters and parcels, is vital to life and business.

And it has become a big business and a cash cow to many nations who had trapped to explore the gains from the advancement in the information and communications and information technology sectors. In all the worlds, it is the most vital in the social technology and engineering. Communications ministry is a management, through the act 2003 establishing Nigerian Communications Commission (NCC), of the communications institutions like the GSM operators, Code Division Multiple Access (CDMA) operators (licensed private and public telecoms firms) and all communications service providers for effective service delivery without shortchanging of the users under any disguise of distortions, extortion, poor and epileptic services. It is therefore a source of generating billions for the nation from the effective managing of the existing telecoms, public and private, improving on the **broadband plan** to **30%** target by **2018** as inherited from the previous administration of **Ms Omobola Johnson** (predecessor Minister of communications between 2011 and 2015). It is necessary to enforce payment of refund of illegal charges and rates to the coffers of government while the subscribers are able to collect theirs back in form of credits and free services as supported by the **act** or its probable amendment that established the communication sector in the advanced economies such as United States, Britain and Germany.

Secondly, the nation could leverage on the improved internet facility provided and CDMA technology to sell different products especially intellectual property from resource people in the nations. Today, United States has over **5,000 libraries** as revealed in the Library Congress of Control Number (LCCN) United Kingdom has over **4,000 libraries**. A type of library that would pave the way for several online businesses is a **DIGITAL ELECTRONIC READING BILLBOARD**. This is knowledge-driven business that would drive the entrepreneurial spirits in undergraduates and post graduates in the national institutions. Nigeria will be pacesetter to have this type across the continents.

Without doubt, this is a business for the Ministry of Communications in collaboration with ministries of education and environment to sponsor as the internet facilities at the beck and call from the operating companies under the ministry's supervision are readily available to promote digital electronic reading billboards. Again, it has to do with collaboration efforts with Ministry of education and Environment to get space allocations where digital electronic billboards would be located and the **locally-generated intellectual materials** from list of professionals and talented Nigerians would be programmed and showcased for the emerging reading environment being created in all tertiary institutions across the nation. Several private operators especially among the youths who are into ICT, arts and other technical courses should also be licensed to add input to the gross domestic products (GDP) and gross national income (GNI).

The commercial aspects of internet entrepreneurs are not limited to the science-based courses but for social science-based courses. Those who have selling skills, marketing, mentoring, and several others could start lucrative business online. Let us assume **1000** are registered as online business companies, and each makes a sale of **5000** items per month at average of **10 dollars** per item (e-book, films, songs, gifts, electronics, advert placement, toys, boutique..). This equals to **50m dollar** sales. 10% Value added tax of **50 million dollar** sales amounts to 5million dollar per month. In exchange rate of 199 naira to a US dollar, it amounts to **995** million naira. In a large market like Nigeria where all other big markets patronize for one thing or the other; whom they know is blessed with natural resources and talents in human resources, it is highly possible for each registered online business in the nation generating up to **5 billion US dollar** worth of goods and services per month. VAT, sales tax, Personal Income tax or pay as you earn, company or corporate taxes among others from dues from the raw materials for local productions would fetch the nation not less than **500m US dollar per month** or **99.500 billion naira per month**! This writer is sure that a writer from Nigeria cannot have less than ten popular books not to talk of the weekly and periodical releases from the film industry and the entertainment sector, fashion houses among others.

COMMUNICATIONS SECTOR IN COLLABORATION WITH EDUCATION MINISTRY TO GENERATE BILLIONS

There are several ways education and communications ministries can partner to boost revenue generation, create lucrative and pensionable employments for thousands from different professional disciplines and increase the degree of reading culture with the potential and resources that are readily available to the nation. Let us look at an example. E-library business service, in form of online library, running lending, reference library and e-book mall online, is like a market departmental store on air space, or shop in the terrestrial markets where variants of educational products and services locally sourced are sold to target customers within and beyond the shores. This is fast becoming one of the sources of income for proprietors across the nations especially in the advanced ICT nations. It is generating millions of jobs for people in the advanced nation which share similar features with Nigeria. The features include the population, the people who have the desires and appetite no matter the purchasing powers to buy things as all-time buyers of limitless needs.

Jovago.com reports on hotel bookings in Nigeria show that e-commerce generates 1.5 billion naira weekly from almost **70% online bookings** (Punch: 54 of August 10 2015). The number of internet users in the biggest market in Africa- Nigeria, is increasing by the day put at present around one hundred million. The proliferation of online marketplaces or retailers like **konga.com, jumia.com** among others has created room for sub-markets such as online libraries. Our research about online retailer in America- **amazon.com** showed that the business had <u>**over 65,000 e-sellers**</u> as at the second quarter of 2012 (Wikipedia); **Barnes and Noble** has **over 900,000 e-sellers** and register in hundreds of school campuses and has its own physical libraries. <u>Nigeria, like US and UK has great potentials to generate several hundreds of thousands of lucrative jobs</u> for the nation.

Nigeria, with the available resources as existing in the advanced economies, cannot be an exception with her intellectual resources and ever booming manpower. From emerging authors, researchers, thesis of the graduates and post-graduates, and tertiary tutors who have publishable materials in all categories of human endeavours to start e-commerce in the online publishing, online library. With these **two major inputs**, the business would generate anticipated results in employment generation and raking in billions in average per month.

This project is aimed at knowledge-driven economy where **digital online bookstores** are established, at least <u>one per state</u>, and stock with books from Nigerian authors and intellectual materials from researches. This would generate employment opportunities for Nigerians and increase the source of IGR to not less than **35 billion naira** <u>per month</u> from the target sale of just **50,000** each for a book in a month from a **50-popular book** on each of the online stores at **$2** per book as gain for the government after paying taxes, salaries and royalties for the owners of the intellectual property. Assuming the Ministry establishes one online station per state with each running under different management. We target **50,000 x 100 x $2 x 37 = $370m**. At an exchange rate of **199 naira** to a US dollar, the nation has the ability to generate **73.630 billion naira** <u>per month</u>. This figure is about **one-seventh** of the monthly figure of the fiscal budget of 2015 over four trillion naira.

All the stations can have similar intellectual materials. We can stock them with several projects and thesis in the libraries from our after passing through quality tests. Fortunately, Nigeria is endowed with thousands of writers whose works are in tens across the regions. In fact, many states and professional bodies can take a cue from this to establish new stores as the cyber space can accommodate all without hitch. One can imagine having THREE government-owned digital online stores and electronic reading billboard specially designed for free readers across the three senatorial zones of each state of the nation. Around **110.445 billion naira** would be generated per month to the coffers of the government. How would an online store generate such quantity of sales in a month? Who would drive the activity as management staff? What are the steps to be taken to attract buyers from within and across global geographic business environment? These are in the urgent inevitable **reforms** specially designed at the tail end of this work for the project (turning the sector into a cash-cow) to become a reality.

Considering the almost one hundred million users of internet in Nigeria (The Nation: 42 of November 2, 2015) through the 4 popular Global System Mobile Communication networks (GSM) and Code Division Multiple Access (CDMA) of Multilinks, Telkoms, Visafone, Spectranet 4g lite, Starcomms, Smile, Scannet et al; the nation has the potential to generate billions from the resources materials each month. The market is large enough.

STEPS TO GENERATE BILLIONS FROM THE INTERNET SERVICE PROVIDERS

The regulatory body has a great role to play to ensure the market is expanded to attract new providers. One of the methods that would be effective is the downward review of operating licenses and get all the users either in retail or wholesale of prepaid and postpaid customers properly documented time to time.

The following steps are equally important to create revenues from internet users at offices, homes and institutions:

Firstly, all the cyber cafes, at home-offices, offices, businesses and institutions must **by enhancing law** from the reviews of the **NCA Act** be properly registered with the NCC as they are registered under the corporate affairs commission (CAC) just like all e-libraries and online business sites.

Secondly, the ISP business license should be allotted places to operate. For instance, some may be licensed to cover certain local government area as against the whole country.

Thirdly, the prices should be moderate enough to attract millions. If a service charge is **three** naira per minute, such may attract **five** million users per month amounting to **fifteen** million naira unlike if the service charge is ten naira per minute and only a million patronize the service amounting to **ten** million naira for the month. The popular mobile networks operators (MNOs) compete with slash prices with different pricing **promotions** and **freebies** to attract more subscribers. Today, over **148 million Nigerians** are claimed to use at least one of the networks (NCC:2015). This has enabled many Nigerian run double, triple and sometimes four sims to meet their need.

Fourthly, all the **sub-sellers** of all the **data** and **credits** should have all their records updated every day since selling and purchasing of credits and data is at every moment. A parent body should register them; where the books of accounts are kept for the NCC inspection rights at the right time. For instance, if **smile.com**, for instance, sells data to **1,000 cafes** and **5,000 private users** and **200 business institutes** in a state; such records of transactions should be stored for public use later by the NCC for the determination of the actual **taxes** and dues of the nation. Failure to keep the record may force the NCC to use another power to **revoke** their license of operation and get it fined accordingly.

Fifthly, software-based codes of loading must be produced by the collaboration of the software engineers of the regulators and the operators in the telecom sector and its affiliates. These codes would serve the purpose of eliminating **taxes**

evasion. Let us use a practical illustration. Keep customers informed to use **x552x2x00xpin#** to load where **552** stands for the network, **2** stands for the account of the network where its own money (selling price less VAT) is transferred and the **00** is the code number for the government VATs from the pin (amount of credits paid for) where **#** is '<u>okay</u>' or agreement to terms and condition of service. Government must do the same for all other revenue generation activities illustrated in the book to prevent diversion of funds to private pockets. Software developers must be employed to develop software to capture the transactions of the services and products where relevant taxes are deducted from the source.

GENERAL GAINS

a) Increase in income from intellectual property and to render the dependence on revenues from oil to the background.
b) Generating VATs and other forms of levies from the source to eliminate shortchanging from the part of the operators and affiliates
c) Increase in the number of ISPs would take the benefits of the services to the nooks and corners of the nation boosting socio-economic activities, research findings and smooth running of political and technological advancement.
d) Several online and offline businesses would start to proliferate with the cost-effective and efficient web services
e) Opportunities would grow with the effectiveness in the internet and telephony services across the length and breadth of the nation and beyond
f) Improvement and proper regulation of the communications ministry and its regulatory agencies would create rooms for more lucrative employments
g) To drive the knowledge-driven economy and attract foreigners into made-in-Nigerian intellectuals resource materials. Foreigners would have deep and better knowledge of the locally produced goods and services

h) Expansion of businesses would be an added values chain to the nation with its multiplier effects to the GDP and GNI.
i) The nation would in no time gains its re-enlistment, into the **JP Morgan** and the likes in the global financial market, as one of the emerging market as a force to be reckoned with the revenues from online business and e-activities.
j) To add values to the intellectual values of the intellectual property owners in the nation and generating hard currencies in millions each month
k) To spread wealth round the people as they can earn without sweat at the comforts of their homes
l) To generate **injections** into the economy for budget finance and improve reading culture
m) It is an opener for the private investors to key into this kind of projects too to increase more jobs and revenues including wealth re-distribution among people; for instance the e-library in tertiary schools could be upgraded to become online bookstores, online markets for specialized products and services.
n) In advanced economies and some neighbouring African nations, public corporations are run side by side (competing) with the private investors. For instance, government has its own schools, hospitals, airlines, research institutions making profits for the nation aside creating employment for the people.

REFLECTION

United States of America, United Kingdom, Germany, China and India among others are creating millionaires every day simply because they patronize home made goods and services. If Nigerians tap a lesson from this. With enough human and natural endowments available in the nation, we should be creating millionaires every day too as we have in the **blueprint**. In addition, wealth would be vastly distributed to several millions of hands. Through the proliferation of online retailers, industrialization is enhanced as most patrons of the local online marketplaces would be the local firms. In this clime, Nigerians have millions of potential online buyers of goods and services with the increasing number of smartphones users with e-reading devices.

DEMERIT OF ONLINE BOOKS SELLERS

a) Inability to get the right records of buyers of the e-product (e-book formats of books) and the supplies of the physical books.
b) Difficulty in the records of the online businesses for proper documentation, control and regulation
c) Difficulty in the tracking of the right VATs charged by the sellers especially those who use manual records for records of sales
d) Challenge of the pirates who could hack the site and get free downloads without making any payment. The support and collaboration of all agencies and the public could only be used to wade off the pirates across the climes (Read details on how to tackle piracy headlong in the book "**Piracy, the trends, the spiral effects and the practicable solutions**" by the same author)

SOLUTION TO THE DEMERITS

The fact is that online business owners especially the **online publishers** are not spirits as they have either real names or pseudonyms, operate in a resident registered under the planning authority even if it is home-office and not offices at business districts meant for such transaction. They operate with phones and mails with websites. They had records of the businesses they had worked with and sometimes some representatives who might have met one time or the other. They would at least have registered business number with government even at local district. They may be operating virtual business and selling on air. They make transfer on air, receive orders on air, direct the printers to print via mails of certain quantity paid for online by customers and the deal is done. They are not difficult to track down and made to pay royalty and taxes to the right authority.

There are steps to track them to pay for their breach of contract and the public trust for evading taxes as anticipated by the nation where they operate.

Firstly, all the online businesses can be traced through the mails, phone contacts and addresses of their bankers, the affiliate business partners. Let us give a good example. An online publishing firm was trying to dupe close author of his royalty. We had the bank account of the company from online interaction since all payment through the account. Owners of the account and their location would be unveiled at the appropriate time by the bank and the publishers' printing press spread across the nations.

Secondly, those marketers they work with have certain knowledge about the firm. The print out from the internet are admissible by court of jurisdiction to prosecute the case. Such reports must be able to show the sales indicators as the information therein shall be used by the prosecuting lawyers before the court. Information like 'bestseller, bestselling, most sold, most popular, hits, sold out.. are not just use carelessly be sellers. They stand for sales for the item.

Thirdly, the sellers know the account they paid to and by tracing these, the identity of the owners are unveiled. In fact, the ISBN tracker at the back of the book could be used to track the number of sales

Fourthly, the distributor agencies like **lightning source** knows how to locate them. On the having the records of sales to avoid tax evasion, efforts with the assistance of software makers are called to task. It is via **developing a software solution** in form of **centralized portal** to track all the records of virtual sales and transactions at all places at the time of transactions. This must involve several regulatory bodies that must work in unison to get all the records by centralize the stores connecting to the account system office of the **online stores**.

As regards the fear of **tax evasion** by the relevant government agencies, especially the online businesses, government should enact laws that would force all the **e-sellers** in collaboration with their service providers to have records of daily sales as correspondingly monitor from the site of the agency. The systems of the company must be connected to those of the agencies for clearer records of purchases. By this, government is in control of the access to websites. And the agencies should also involve the software engineers of the service providers for records purposes. By so doing, **trillions of naira** could be generated as Internally Generated Revenues to the treasury of the nation from tracking the **online sales taxes** and **vats** and if the nation could support the tertiary institutions to sell their intellectual property to earn money for the institutions and the nation. (Read **"Zero tolerance to taxes by all businesses"** in a book to be published later)

EXPERIENCES SHARED FROM SUBSCRIBERS

From the first experience, almost all the subscribers to all forms of communications networks have one complain or the other especially in the aspect of cheating the ignorant, docile and passive customers. Credits and data are removed from the subscribers' accounts without justification in most cases. There is always loss of signals and network services, which in most cases, ruin the lives and property of the subscribers. Let us share some experience of clients:

"I used to enjoy a service from my network provider. One day, I loaded a credit and immediately the credit was removed. I tried to make a call after loading, but a voice message from the network said that I had no credit to make the call. It was annoying. I checked my balance and found out that there was no credit again to call as claimed. I instantly contacted the customer care hotline. After several minutes of not less than thirty, it was picked. The staff told me that the credit was removed in payment for the subscription of a caller tune I had made. And sincerely, I had never subscribed to any caller tunes".

"A message was sent to my phone that I should answer a question by selecting one of the options given to win certain sum of money. The question was simple. I picked the right answer. And it was responded with a message that I had scored and my charge of fifty naira had been deducted for participation. When I tried to reach out to my network operators, they claim ignorance. I later got to know that it was the making of the value added service operators".

"I paid subscriptions for my cable television. Unfortunately, the epileptic supply of electricity did not allow me to watch the stations of choices till the subscriptions got expired. I had to buy another subscription for another month. The second month, the cable station did not perform as anticipated for several loss of signals in transmissions. All efforts to make the operators to formally apologize not to talk of compensating me proved abortive. I later learnt I wasn't the only victim."
"My case is different. I subscribed to a promotion plan. When the network deducted certain sum of money from my account, I became a subscriber or beneficiary of certain credits. What I noticed was that the free credits got exhausted than the normal credits that I used to buy before entering into the promotional tariff plan. I made some efforts to record the seconds and minutes of calls from the network to the same network, and the network to other networks, I found out that the charges had increased at all times, not just the peak and off-peak periods."

"I did not subscribe to a code and the operator used to send me messages every day. At the end of the month, my account balance was reduced by 50 naira. On enquiry that took over 30 minutes before the online customer care officer could attend, I was told that I had subscribed to the code which I never did. The woman at the customer care told me to type 'stop' and send to the number of the code. And this was the time it was stopped. How many subscribers would care to go thus far? And yet no compensation".

TRACKING THE OPERATORS CHEATS ON SUBSCRIBERS AND GENERATING BILLIONS PER MONTH AS FAIR CHARGES FOR SUBSCRIBERS AND THE NATION

We cannot talk about how to eliminate cheating tendencies of the MNOs without proper listing of their bad business activities. It is common for operators to charge the subscribers under illicit **'terms and conditions'** hidden to the subscribers and the deductions from the value added services providers that use short codes. Many a subscriber lose credits to unsubscribed caller-tunes forced down on their throats, epileptic services (of digital television and radio stations especially of the pay per view stations) that are faulting are paid for, many a time credits purchased with hard-earned money loaded that are not credited and refunded, poor customer service, unlicensed bloggers depriving the people, places and institutions their rights from illicit publication and online messes like cyber-crimes...., indiscriminate charges which are hike without the notice of the subscribers, unsolicited messages that drop the calls, call drops during business and at the peak of urgent discussion, pending messages, undelivered messages, telecommuting service due to poor service causing inestimable loss at different places leading to loss of livelihood, lives and several other assets....

In view of the manners of cheats being perpetuated by the licensed and the unlicensed operators (MNOs, ISPs, VAS providers, the subscribers are looking for change in the sector and desire payment for the defaulting services. There are ways to track them and get the dues for them and the nation as penalty fees instead of slamming whopping sum on them. The operators may challenge the penalty at the floors of the court. With what we have as template to capture the actual defaults and the costs to the subscribers, the operators would wake up to their social and business responsibility. Let us cite some facts as regards the shortchanging of the subscribers of their money. A MNO charge for a promotion platform used to be **20Kobo** for calls from the same brand, and the same charges **50 Kobo** for each second for all other networks connection. For s**pending any message**, a sum of **four naira** would be charged. And the machine has been programmed in a way that it deducts the amount immediately the message is sent but undelivered. If the records of the subscribers being shortchanged on undelivered messages **per week** from the records of each network are properly documented through certain **portal**, not less than 20 million out of an average of 30m users would have claims from the service providers. Let us do this

Mathematically. **20m x 4 x 4 MNOs x 4weeks** in a month=**1280m** or **1.28 billion** naira per month for the pending messages for the **FOUR** most popular MNOs.

If the drop calls accounted for **60 million per month** amounts to **.25 x 60m=15m naira**. The sales come from different forms of baits as promotions from the most viable four MNOs. For instance, a network would advertise that buy **100 credits** and enjoy **200% free credits** for a specify number of days. If such customer has been one that spends one hundred naira for three days before, he would move up to talk more. Once this habit goes on for a month, he would not be able to cut the credits for calls again that he will be indirectly 'forced' to buy more. Those who are used to make calls of one thousand per week would grow to buying three thousand naira later. The trend among the consumers would continue unabated.

There is the inevitable need to **develop a template** by the ICT section of the NCC connected to the supervisory ministry as a back-up that would capture who is deprived (names of the subscribers deprived of the credits or bytes) and the MNO that deprived such (with names and location), how (method), where (place) and when (time and date) such was deprived, in what way he/she was deprived and the cost of the deprivation. The subscribers (person, institute or business) would **have their credits return** at the end of each month and **the illicit money** in the coffers of the operators would be refunded to the purse of the government.

REASONS TO TRACK THE POOR SERVICES

Nigerian Communications Commission (NCC) has over **100m** registered Global System of Mobile communication network SIM card users and over 93% internet users with CDMA. If a network has its 50m subscribers who are deprived an average of 100 minutes call per month, it amounts to **.20 per second x 100 x 50m x 4** (popular mobile networks owners -Globacom, Etisalat now 9mobile, MTN, Airtel) = **4 billion naira** (Four Billion Naira). What about the defunct Visafone and Multilinks telkoms, Mtel, helios, zoom, o'net, medallion, monacom, webcom, starcomms et al? It is a fact that customers that are over 50m are deprived for more than 100 minutes per month from field studies and interviews. One can imagine the penalty to government coffers and refund of the charges to the affected clients by **legislative act** of the national assembly.

The poor network service has deprived people, places and events, for instance, delays in passengers flights to take off for different issues- business, social et al; many depositors at banks wander at banks; and several other ways to deprive people, businesses, institutions and the nation, security of lives and property get difficult with bad network service of connecting network at the time of emergency and for the surveillance CCTV and **centralized portals** where available et al.

From the earlier chapter, the fines to serve as deterrents to others have shown the ministry better way to generate billions from the offenders. It is a reform that would sanitize the communications sector of the nation. In fact, the nation is able to generate almost **285 billion naira per month** from reports of vices alone. Let us imagine the amount if the penalty on the illicit services of the MNOs and ISPs.

What about the penalty on drop calls, unsolicited messages, extortion of the highest order from the unsubscribed for caller tunes charges deducted epileptic services and extortions of the digital television and radio stations among others. What about the number of hours of service loss for the internet users at all industries in all sectors? What about the defaults of all other communication outfits especially Internet Service Providers (**ISPs**) that buys bulk gigabytes from the licensees like scannet.com, ipnx, spectranet 4g lite, smile.om, yudala.com and such online retailers that depend on the internet service like jumia.com, konga.com, kaymus.com among others, serving the business cafes in their thousands, financial institutions hospitality business, transportation business, educational activities, manufacturing and all strata of social and economic lives not to talk of the millions of private users performing below expectation?

REASONS WHY SLAMMING HUGE PENALTY IS UNFAIR TO THE SERVICE PROVIDERS

1) The huge fine may result in the scaling down of staff via retrenchment and outright loss of jobs of Nigerians working with them. Loss of jobs would add to the scourge of unemployment in the nation and hence becomes a threat to lives and property.
2) The firms would continue to rip the subscribers the more since they know it will be penalty as usual.

N.B. This project sees it as **unfair** slamming whopping fines on the telecoms operators in order to avoid sending them out of business and its negative ripple effects on the socio-economic wellbeing of the nation and nationals, the **template** designed to track the poor runs of services shall be the right tool to make them pay for the defaulting services.

THE OPERATORS HAVE REASONS FOR POOR SERVICES

Reasons abound why there is probable poor services from the side of the operators. Some of these are illustrated below:

a) Inadequate finance to pay adequate number of quality staff to management their facilities
b) The vandals who vandalize their installation especially in the hot zones.
c) Lack of enough manpower from within to manage the modern machines
d) Huge money as graft to enjoy running of the business by the official of government and the impersonators.

GENERATING BILLIONS FROM COLLABORATION WITH TRANSPORT MINISTRY

In the modern day of transportation system, the roads, the rails and the seas can become **crime-free** with installation of communication devices. The fines on offenders of users would attract billions from the collections from all the facilities across the nation. Let us use a simple mathematical calculation. If the number of road offenders (over-driving, neglect of road signs, street fighting, litters of the roads, bribe givers, dangerous driving, disobedience to traffic lights) captured by the surveillance camera per state is 10,000 per month and each is made to pay an average fine of **20,000 naira;** the nation will be generating **20,000 x 10,000= 200,000,000 naira** per state per month. The 37-state nation is target at generating **200 m x 37=7,400 million or 7.4 billion naira per month**!

In addition, all road tax in form of toll fees should be collected through e-payment system. POS machine should be placed at the toll to prevent collection through ticket.

ANOTHER SOURCE OF GENERATING REVENUES FROM NIPOST OF THE COMMUNICATION MINISTRY

Effective postal and courier services in advanced economy like United States make the amazon.com and others are making success of their online retailing businesses. Several affiliates of these businesses have taken source from the growth and expansion of amazon.com barnes and noble et al. In Nigeria, the institution started in the 19th century when six post offices were established in Ibadan, Badagry, Ijebu-Ode, Abeokuta, Epe and Ikorodu. Royal air force took the first international mail from Kano to Cairo in 1925. Decree of Jan 1, 1985 that established Nigerian Telecommunications (NITEL) gave birth Nigerian Postal service department. The decree of 1987 gave powers to NIPOST. Many post offices were established across the federation. Today, owing to the liberalization of the sector, private courier and logistic services have joined the service. With the trend of growth, the restructuring of the post offices and courier services is an inevitable.

The need to go digital can be more profitable competing with private-owned courier services like Express mail services, red logistics, DHL, Cargo express et al. The internet service can be used to create better offline and online offices for the state-owned institution (NIPOST) under the ministry. The courier services are more patronized than the public owned NIPOST from studies. It takes initiation of promotional strategies in massive advertisements and freebies to sell the services of the institutions to the people, places, institutions et al. the space is too large for all of them in similar business to generate right number of clients and generate billions per month. The institution should be run like the private operators who work on set targets. We have designed **ways** for the postal service management to be earning more money from their services.

GAINS

1. It puts the operators, both private and public, on their toes to improve on their track of performance and makes the administration of all public and private businesses be more effective and efficient.
2. It helps to avoid cheating of the subscribers of the operators and generate billions for the nation from refunds of the illegally collected charges to the

coffers of the government and refund of the services to the consumer as a way to protect the consumer rights over the defaulting firms

3. The epileptic services that may be traced to substandard phones may be a good case for the improvement of the manufacturers of the phones for quality productions.
4. It sanitizes the system in a way that more entrepreneurs would find the nation as a right environment to invest since their telecoms interests have been protected.
5. All businesses- banks, airports, seaports, research institutions, private businesses, media stations, government MDAs et al would enjoy near perfect services for the service charges
6. And more capable hands would be employed by the operators to have adequate number of technical staff members to man all the service stations and masts at all nooks and corners of the federation. More staffs mean that employments would be created.
7. The 'change mantra' would have added values by the effective and efficient operation of the telecoms institutions for the ruling party to retain its foremost place as a trailblazer in the political terrain of the nation cum the continent.

REVENUE GENERATIONS

1. The nation shall earn from the refunds of the charges as well as the customers that would be refunded with the exact free services they were deprived of.
2. With the powers such as the prescription of the amount of postage stamps and exploring of other means to generate revenues to the coffers, the agency has several innovations to borrow from the private operators in order to make greater profits. Today, all investors are bound by law to fix stamps on their papers to generate incomes for the service.
3. There would be sanity in the system and the nation as the right environment to operate businesses.

4. Both online and offline postal services would generate more money for the nation including the employment of more people.

COMMMUNICATIONS SECTOR IN COLLABORATION WITH DEFENCE MINISTRY TOWARDS GENERATING BILLIONS

All ministries must work in synergy to ensure general administration. One of the essential ministries that communications ministry must work with is the **Ministry of Defence** and of **interior. Security of lives and property** is significant to the national developments and the security agents must be at other places to render better security covers. The facilities being in the custody of communications ministry would aid the security stability in the nation if telecoms owners are contracted per local government to install close circuit television or surveillance cameras at the highways, business districts, malls, private and public-owned institutions. The installation, by **all the tiers of government** in particular and businesses (including charity-based institutions) of Close Circuit Television (CCTV) at strategic places and **connected to centralized portals** would reduce the services of the security forces (agents) to man offices, gridlocks and robber attacks roads and institutions especially the airports 'swindlers and spies', seaports 'rats'. Aside this gain, revenues would be generated from the offenders and the crime rates would be drastically reduced across the length and breadth of the nation. Employments would be generated for Nigerians as builders and maintainer of all the projects.

COMMUNICATIONS SECTOR IN COLLABORATION WITH MINISTRY OF TRANSPORTATION AND INTERIOR

The degree of **impunity** and corruption would end with the working together of the ministries identified with the communications ministry. One can imagine if the surveillance camera being monitored by private security institutions would do in the customs, prisons and borders at all ports. Piracy, smuggling, cross border crimes and tax evaders would be highly checked and probably eliminated with the devices in strategic places. If the nation is realizing **ten billion naira** from the custom before this, this author believes that not less than **fifty billion naira** would be generated at the same period. This also goes for the other part of security outfits.

PART FOUR

TROUBLESHOOTINGS: CAUSES AND PRACTICABLE SOLUTIONS

In the light of what we have read in the course, we could understand the plight of the subscribers and the nation in the communications sector such as **epileptic services** at **exorbitant charges**, shortchanging among others. The following are the identified causes:

a) <u>Understaffing</u>: Most of the licensed operators of different classes of licenses do not have adequate staff to manage their reach. Some may not have adequate technical staff to run the heavy machines and installations. Government-owned public sector has poorly organized staff members who are not given set standard of output.

b) <u>Inadequate reach</u>: Most of the firms do not have mast and interconnectivity gadgets at the right places of needs especially the rural and remote places and geographical areas. Most drop calls and loss of signal and services are due to this problem which has caused inestimable loss to the people such as loss of irreplaceable human lives and property worth billions.

SOLUTIONS

a) Solve understaffing by procurement of competent and adequate technical staff to manage the infrastructures
b) Expand the business service reach through the creation of several mast stations and effectively equip them with staff and equipment relevant to drive the mission and objectives
c) Demand for feedbacks from the subscribers-clients to redress abnormally, technical or human errors and mistakes
d) Delisting or blacklisting of the under-performing licensees or set a standard for them with set time

THE FIVE-PRONGED REFORMS

To correct all the institutional ills, make billions as IGR and creating jobs for millions as illustrated in the chapters, there is need for perfection of the **human and institutional reforms** through the patriotic collaboration efforts of the executive, the judiciary and the legislative arms of government with the support of the activists and the statesmen in the council of state. Also needed to contribute inputs are the specialized technical consultants and media gurus who would formulate the reforms to drive the communications sector to achieve the desire goal. **Reforms** by **acronym**, we mean

R: regulate, revamp, revitalize, resuscitate and reviews regulatory powers where and when necessary

E: Emancipate, enhanced lives and business with improved policies and incentives

F: fuse things via adequate formulation of ideas towards connectivity at all times and places with the use of patriotic specialized technocrats

O: Organize all inputs to gain all desired outputs at set or standard time at all places on merits and not on the basis of federal character

R: renovate, re-invent new solutions and reinvigorate by declaration of emergency in the sectors

M: moving each of the sectors forward with the apps produced by patriotic and selfless experts

S: success of all facets of life of staff, subscribers and the national integrity at sight

BRIEF HINTS ABOUT THE MNOs

Reforms are inevitable on the basis of the hints about the licensees. Some of the hints to know about the MNOs are:

a) MNOs are the sellers of the data services in retail and bulk for internet users (Private and business-oriented buyers)
b) MNOs sell credits as pre-paid and postpaid to different buyers
c) MNOs always partner with value added service (VAS) providers.
d) Most of the MNOs compete with different data and tariff plans to retain subscribers
e) They are investing to have greater reach and expanding through partnering with others as recently done by Globacom with Vodafone.

These social **reforms** are divided into **five** with the supports of the three arms of government namely:

a) <u>For the ministry</u>: Recognitions should be given to the demands of relevant stakeholders such as Nigerian Society of Computers (NSC), Association of Licensed Telecoms (ALTON)… with what it obtains as global standard practices. All the powers of the NCC should wear new looks and clearly re-defined to achieve national objective. The staff members at each of the state capital office must be re-orientated on the new challenges. This induction must be done to read out riot act to the managers of all the anticipated messages from all stakeholders. No messages via mails, voice, telex, fax, must be treated with utmost urgency and privacy of the senders must be protected. **Punitive measures** against defaulting staff should be communicated. It is expected that all messages must be collated, analyzed, sorted out and dispersed to the real owners and such must be copied to the higher authority for proper monitoring and overall supervision. There should be checks and balances by separate desks in the office for different contents. There should be an <u>agreed code in the jointly-prepared subscribers loading software</u> where all deductions are shared at the point of sales or purchase. In other case, government representatives, like the party agents at the polling units for party under the **electoral laws**, working in the sales department as supervisor, must counter-sign manually and by electronic to confirm what is sold in **credits** and **bytes** for subscribers with records of retail and bulk sales of the retail and bulk prepaid and postpaid buyers and at what prices at what time for easy computation and deduction of taxes especially the value added taxes and personal income taxes and other due levies per month since the corporate sales taxes and some others are declared at the end of the annual general meetings. This reform is taken from the powers which are **to approve the guidelines** <u>for keeping accounts</u> and cost allocation formula of licensees; and regular summoning the licensees over the services, VAT and other taxes.

b) <u>For the regulatory agency</u>: All the agencies under the ministry must be tasked or re-tasked towards meeting the new **change mantra**. It is the nationals and the nation first. The 'terms and conditions' on products and of services to the subscribers must have inputs of the agency in order to eliminate the shortchanging of the subscribers by the operators under the unkind conditions. All terms and conditions must wear human face and not that of inhumane 'capitalists'. The Nigerian Communications Commission (NCC) is having more works on its shoulders as revealed in the number of the licensed operators under different classes. There should be separated agency for different classes especially the Value Added Services (VAS) providers that are making money with no proper accountability. All the **licensees** should be allotted standard of performance. Let there be a separate regulators for the MNOs and another for ISPs. By this step, it is anticipated that work overloads or transfers to the other times would be different from the past. The agency should post aftermaths of each report worked upon from the right agencies or ministries to serve as feedback on the website and digital media handles of the ministry every week latest. People and businesses would be served right if the websites and twitter or other social media handles get daily updates. Place the analyzed and confirmed reports with fact on the site without the names of the senders to keep its privacy right intact. The agency must review its powers on the issuing of licenses and regular summoning of the MNOs over epileptic services and the imposition of illicit terms and conditions hidden to the customers. The body should review or redefine the powers of determination of principles to guide interconnection arrangement between operators and also the determination of services and new undertaking eligible for licensing from time to time. All operators must be guided by a set standard of global telecom operation standard.

c) <u>Telecoms market and stakeholders reforms</u>: Each licensed telecoms and defined subsidiaries by the communication ministry particularly the Nigerian Communications Commission as powered by **NC Act 2003** to with set objectives and powers on telecom and other classes of licenses should be mandated by NCC to present the actual number of the registered and unregistered customers or subscribers in a universal software or a portal to synergize their activities. This is transparency. Also, all phone makers and customized sellers or distributors should comply with certain reforms to <u>make</u> (manufacturing), <u>import</u> and <u>sell</u> quality phones and their accessories. All MNOs and ISPs should publish their transactions every month with necessary data to ascertain what is spent by each user of the network and for what (call, text, transfers, payments…). The sector should by law made to publish the reasons why there is hike in tariff at a particular time or the causes of epileptic services are happening. And how much is paid to the named treasury agency of the government should be published to ensure **transparency and accountability** on the part of the firms to the public. It is a fact that billions can be generated from the operation per month if the reforms take the right shape.

d) <u>Reforms for other ministries, departments and agencies</u>: All MDAs must have ethical guides for all the staff members. The guides must be produced in the major languages and the lingua franca (English language) in an **unambiguous sentence**. The ministries should also open receiving units where the messages received are also analyzed and disseminated to the right users without delay. Let us explain this by some illustrations. Assuming a **report** is got that dumps of refuse are at a particular place was sent to the environment ministry through the communications ministry alert, the former should act by sending the department under it to be up to task to ensure garbage-free environment. If the ministry of finance got a message that certain taxes from a company on VAT is supposed to be **2m naira** and the amount remitted is **1m naira** from **xyz company**, then all the departments and agencies especially Federal Inland Revenue Service (FIRS) must be notified to commence investigation over the issue. There should be a back-up that would serve as checks and balances to put all on their toes. The time of sending the reports, the receivers and the next line of action should be sent as reply to the reports got in form of acknowledgement. When a **report on tax evasion** is received by the Ministry of Finance, its affiliated agencies from the communications ministry, the acknowledgement duly dated and signed must be sent to the latter as acknowledgement for record purpose.

e) Reforms of the citizens or stakeholders (local and foreigners): The Communications ministry should propose reforms to check the unsubstantiated reporters from flooding their units with such illicit and blasphemous reports. Public **i-reporters** should be taught ethics guiding how to present their documents and reports to prevent those who have taken it up as employment. The protocols and quorum must be observed to avoid the raising sentimental alerts. Recently, there was a sponsored bill of the national assembly on the 2nd of December by a national assembly Senator, the Deputy Senate Leader, Bala Ibn Na'llah from the ruling APC (2015-2019), where penalties of two years jail terms and four million or two millions fine option for libelous and abusive publications without taking oaths by people online, inside prints, media stations, text messages or posts on the social media handles like twitter, instagram, facebook, whatspp et al are recommended if passed. The bill was aimed at preventing the false alerts or reports from the public users and contributors but the **freedom of information bill** Act where the **right to speech** and **expression of minds** are respected. The content of the act should be communicated with lucid languages and passed through working (effective) media to the public hence the reporters (senders) would abide with in order to refrain from giving false alerts.

BOMBSHELL: GAINS FROM THE REFORMS OF THE SECTOR ON THE NATION

The **reforms** would make <u>tracking the sales of the operators</u> to commensurate with the amount being paid as taxes. Let us give a simple common sense Arithmetic showing how the reforms would have direct positive impacts into the GDP and GNI hence the standard of living. As regards tracking the sales of the operators, field studies show that many literate Nigerians have at least **four popular networks** probably for private and business uses. **Students**, not working class, have <u>at least three</u> even a percentage of the early education pupils have phones. Illiterate market men and women mostly have at least one. In normal days at the moment, network charges.**50 naira** or **fifty kobo per second** call to other networks. As earlier discussed, each of them 'lure' subscribers into using more minutes to call through different **promotional tariff plans**, **data bundles** and unlimited **freebies**(like free night calls, free calls to friends and families, free e-books, free mobile customized phones display messages) to have more social networking discussants. Users of certain network could enjoy a more reduced cost to make longer minutes of calls. Imagine a user whose calls charge are dropped from fifty kobo to twenty kobo. This is tempting to the callers or users of the network to start calling more than before till <u>addiction as culture is cultivated and imbibed</u>. Once the call **addiction** is cultivated as a habit, they would not mind spending their feeding allowances on credits. Many users who have less than **100 connects** could have more than **200** with the freebies being used as baits. If we assume that we have active population of 145 million Subscribers Identity Mobile cards on different phone brands for a purpose put as average of users' intention to use the products and services of the MNOs, then the total of **145 x 4 million (580 Million** different **uses)**. If, by assumption from <u>the rate of promotional hypes and freebies</u> as baits to users, each artisanal subscriber buys average of **400naira credits per month**, Nigerian mobile telecoms sector is assumed to be generating about **232 billion naira per month** on calls and text messages alone. One should consider the **credits** for all social media activities (social, economic and political) and personal convectional business calls, charges for bulk short message services among others by others average and above average people and businesses in the nation.

AND THE STUDIES CONFIRM….

On moderate note, with the consuming level of the nationals by field studies, <u>it is not propaganda</u> to assume that all Nigerian and non-Nigerians subscribers with **average of four networks** meant for <u>different purposes namely</u> for **browsing** internet in search of information, socialization, self-development and for limitless other purposes, for **communications** via calling, texting, chatting; for **transferring of data**, bulk and short messages and for **downloading** and **uploading** bulk and retail data, be it under **business, politics** and **social** needs. Our studies show subscribers in the nation in average spend an **average mean of** <u>9000 naira</u> on **credits** and **data plan** <u>per month </u>(See the **table** below) making the sales to be around **5,220,000 million or 5 trillion, 220 billion naira per month**!

TABLE 2

SUBSCRIBERS BY CLASS	CREDITS PURCHASE/Month (N)
Students (average)	1,000.00
Students (above average)	2,500.00
Artisans (below average)	1,500.00 (rural dwellers inclusive)
Artisans (Average and above)	6,000.00
Salary earners (below & average)	3,000.00
Salary earners (above average)	6,000.00
Executives (Business/VIPs)	10,000.00
Politicians	20,000.00

Non-Nigerians (investors) offices inclusive)	20,000.00	(intercom fees for homes and
Business cafes/offices	20,000.00	
	N90,000.00 (Ninety thousand naira)	

The average is 90,000 divided by 10 categories of subscribers making 9,000 (NINE THOUSAND NAIRA) as **average** of money spent per month for calls and other listed uses.

The Mathematical illustration shows **9,000 x 580 million= 522 billion naira per month**!

The ten percent of the sales as value added tax would provide the nation with **522 billion naira** (Five hundred and twenty two billion naira) per month.

Key indicators:

Subscribers are picked from the field studies conducted for a week. Some were contacted directly for oral interview. We had to get information from the domestic staff of some. They were generally picked at random representing each class of segmented users of the networks. Our respondents under different subscribers claimed to spend a minimum of 250 naira per week for the low income earners and students and the aged who mostly depend on their parents, guardians and family members especially working siblings. Most of the big guns used postpaid credits and data services for internet uses. Only the closest staff members volunteered to give a bit information about the amount of credits being loaded per week by the few prepaid subscribers among them.

GENERATING REVENUES IN BILLIONS PER MONTH FROM THE INFORMATION SECTOR

Our efforts to get relevant information on all the radio, cable and satellite television operators proved abortive not to talk of the subscribers. However, a rough estimate of the subscribers of **Multichoice**-owned DSTV was about 10 million as at the last quarter of the year published report in Nigeria. This is a disputable figure as majority of the offices-private and public-owned connect to the cable television. Many individuals, of which no record has been revealed throughout the search, use at least **two** different subscriptions on DSTV, GoTv and NTA/China owned Startimes and the minimum charge per month is one thousand naira for minimum subscription. Many have as high as 10,000 naira subscription fees per month to cover higher cable television stations. And majority who are the poor and the average people, offices, institutions pays a minimum of 1,000 naira per month. We could confirm the number of houses from National Population Commission (NPC) site. Studies confirms that many below average and the average people prefer to build and live in flat or self-contained apartment to living in the all-rooms houses in the densely populated slums and unplanned areas of states. Each rented flat used to have a cable station to enjoy their privacy to the fullest. Our field studies breakdown show that a minimum of cable television is installed and monthly subscribed for in home-offices two in face-to-face one-storey building houses that highly populated the land; one cable station per flat, one per private and public office. Below is a table based on assumption as no empirical data is available for use as at the time of compiling this as guides:

TABLE 3

HOUSE/TYPE (N)	AVE/STATE	CABLE STATION	AVE/SUBSCRIPTION
All rooms	10 m	2	5,000
Flat	25 m	50 m	5,000
Offices	<u>50 m</u>	<u>50 m</u>	<u>2,500</u>
	<u>85 m</u>	**<u>102 m</u>**	**<u>12,500</u>**

The offices include the installations in home-offices, industries, public located offices and institutions, public and private-owned like banks, insurance firms, schools, hospitals, MDAs, foreign exchange parallel market, shopping malls, fuel stations, hotels and hostels among others. The above arithmetically show that the cable stations are earning **6250 x 85 million=531,250 million naira subscriptions** per month! And a 10% VATs which include the withholding taxes amounts to **53,125 million naira** or **53.125 billion naira** from each state in the 36-state nation! With this estimate, the nation would generate unimaginable sum from the collection of **almost two trillion naira per month**!

NB. The above could be used as a projection of what is obtainable after the proper enumeration of the elements involved in the computation. A fact is that the nation has huge potential to generate several billions annually, at least, from the deduction at source of the VATs from the places and time of procurement.

On a lighter rate considering the **economic downturn** scaling down the numbers of subscribers and subscriptions per month, we assume that only **fifty million** are the users and effective payers of monthly subscriptions for the services adding up all the users in offices, institutions, privately and for commercial purposes like the soccer viewing stations, play stations et al. and the average charge per month is approximately put at **5,000 naira**. The nation should be targeting not less than **50m x 5,000** as revenues for the stations. The **VATs** from the revenues, at 10%, shall be **25 billion naira** per month per state. This would fetch into the nation's coffers a total sum of **25 x 36 states** excluding the Federal Capital Territory (FCT), Abuja making **900 billion naira per month**!

OTHER SOURCES OF EARNING REVENUES WITH APPS

GENERATING BILLIONS FROM THE ENERGY SECTOR

At the absence reliable data to have the number of means of transportation in the nation, the assumption fuel consumption levels per kilometer or per week especially of commercial transportation is used. We observed the number of moving vehicles, airplanes running commercial flights and other means of transportation that are buying fuels every day. A fact is that VAT is charged on every litre of fuel. And millions of litres of fuels per week that must pay at least 5% VATS each week. Imagine the use of electronic pay to pay for fuels at the point of transactions by legislation especially at the loading places or depots where the fuels are lifted and such expenses have their VATs deducted by a dedicated app at source. The nation shall earn billions as VATs from the procurement every week.

TABLE 4

VATS FROM CABLE STATIONS SUBSCRIPTIONS PER STATE (per month)

CATEGORY	NUMBER	SUBSCRIPTION CHARGES
All room-house/offices	**2million**	**2,000**
Block of flats/estates	1million	3,500
Institutions of sizes & types	1million	3,000
TOTAL	4 MILLION	**8,500**

5% VAT of 4m multiply by 8500 gives **1.47 billion** per month per state. **37-state nation** (adding the FCT) gives 1.47x37 equal **62.9 billion naira per month**. Mobile viewing stations, online betting and some other mobile users are not part of the above but all transactions can be captured with the use of **apps**.

TABLE 5

VATS ON ADVERTISEMENTS ON PRINT AND ELECTRONIC MEDIA ACROSS THE NATION

CATEGORY	DESCRIPTION	DAILY (N)	MONTHLY (N)
Newspapers	online and offline	50million	1500million

Magazines online & offline	20million	600million
Radio & TV ditto	20million	600million
cable stations online	20million	600million
social media/blog ditto	5million	150 million
outdoor+online markets ditto	5million	150 million
TOTAL		**3600 million**

5% vat of the 3.6 billion would amount to 180 million naira per month

FACTS: Newspaper adverts rate run to over **20 million naira** for full wrap cover coloured pages, **over two million naira** of centerspread and several thousand of naira for black and white adverts (see **Saturday Punch of April 9, 2016 page 7** for **rates exclusive of 5% vats**). Most of the newspapers used to have over 10 pages of adverts per day from our research. One can imagine the millions of VATs that must be earned per day. They also run online adverts for other goods and services for different prices. **Apps** would capture the actual amount being generated monthly and the VATs being evaded. Government can also generate billions from digital advertisements and e-reading billboards at tertiary institutions with our ideas as guides.

HOUSE, OFFICES AND OTHER PHYSICAL STRUCTURES CENSUS

The number of houses, institutions, business ventures, factories and other structures must be provided by the census office for the bureau of statistics for plans. One of the facilities that is an essential to all is electricity. Every consumer pays VATs on the electricity consumption every month. The payment by the use of prepaid card or paper estimate bill notwithstanding. The amount being charged shall run into several billions.

VATS ON ELECTRICITY SECTOR OF THE ECONOMY

The earlier table assumed for the census of the structures can be used to calculate the estimates for VATs of the electricity consumed at different periods. Subscribers for the electricity as an essential **product** are at every homes, offices and stations (places, events and institutions). At the absence of housing census to estimate the number of offices and homes, at least the nation cannot have less than 300 million users altogether.

However, by the recent studies from interviews with the estates managers, revelations from the horse's mouths show that the minimum charge for the private user in a three-room apartment is **6,000 naira per month**. And the commercial users at markets are almost double the amount from research not to talk of industries, factories, institutions, hotels… that are paying hundreds of thousands in a month. We pick average charge of **10,000 naira per month**. Using the **10,000 to multiply 300 million**, we have 3,000,000 million or 3 trillion naira as earnings for the distribution companies per month. **5% of the amount** would give 3 trillion divided by 20 making **150 billion naira per month**!

N.B. It is apparently impossible to get the approximate estimates of sales of companies especially the publishing firms, the entertainment industry and several manufacturing businesses unless there is a law that must compel them to open their books for the tax authority. We cannot make any right assumptions in this case even though the products from the firms in the industries are used by several hundreds of millions. On the part of the entertainment industry, they run adverts for different products and services. We are still working on how to get the estimates of the payable VATs from the firms. The nation can equally make income from the use of whistleblowers who have the resources to say it as it is.

This efforts, aside being money-earning ventures, for both the whistleblowers and the nation, it could eliminate all vices from the nation. Below is a modified table of offences from first-time offenders that must attract heavy fines instead of wasting scarce resources in litigation:

TABLE 6

OFFENCE	NO OF CASES	FINE	TOTAL
PIPELINE VANDAL	100	1 M	100 M
TRANSFORMER-vandal	200	1 M	200 M
FUEL DIVERSION	200	1 M	200 M
CALIBRATED METER	200	1 M	200 M
HIKE PUMP PRICES	200	1 M	200 M
FUEL ADULTERATION	100	.5M	50 M
CONTRABAND SMUGGLER	1000	1 M	1 BN
FAKERY OF DRUGS, DRINKS & FOODS	1000	1 M	1 BN
FAKERS (OTHERS FILMS, BOOKS…)	1000	1 M	1 BN
STEALING BY TRICK (419)	100	10 M	1 BN
LOOTING & RELATED	100	1M	100 M
PUBLIC NUISANCE	1000	.2 M	200 M
ENVIRONMENT pollution	2,000	.05 M	100 M

N.B. Government could increase the list with right fines but with the legislative endorsement in Acts of assembly assented to by the President to scale down the fines or jack them up. The whistleblowers who uploaded the story with facts and figures including the interviews, the pictures and right descriptions to the right authority for quick intervention to nip the ills by the bud shall be entitled to at least 10% of the amount of fine! And his or her identity must be in secret. One can imagine the **billions of naira** the nation will be generating from i-reporting and the **hundreds of thousands of jobs** that would be created in whistleblowing job!

NIGERIA CAN GENERATE BILLIONS OF DOLLARS FROM INTELLECTUAL PROPERTY

Nigeria, like many nations that are underdeveloped or developing across the continents, is blessed with intellectual resources from the pens of writers, findings of researchers, artistic demonstrations of the thespians and singers, drawings of the artists and sculpt of the sculptors, cultural festivals and arts can be exported for the investors and tourists. If the research-based books and theses (projects) from institutions are tapped, collected and branded for exports, billions of dollars are accruable to the coffers of the nation annually. This is a better replacement as a source of forex to the oil sales.

PARTING THOUGHT

One can now imagine what the nation would earn as **VAT** and **other taxes** from the huge sales from the inputs of the innovations from the communications and information sectors. Nations can continually improve on the revenue base as the creativity to open new sectors keeps increasing.

In the tables, we have identified the additional sources from different classes of licensees especially of over two hundred million subscribers to cable stations!

Subscriptions, for cable television, are like the call credits to phones by all subscribers. Studies show that, calls credits and data sell most at places like stadiums, entertainment arena, hotels at weekends and month ends; and also highly patronized where hospitality business takes place, the hostels, the parks, the malls, the markets, the industrial areas, business districts, the schools especially tertiary institutions, and research stations aside those mobile subscribers on their mobile electronic devices, millions of homes, play-stations, soccer viewing centres, sports betting and lotteries. hotels, research stations and schools, offices-public and private, institutes et al. They, willingly and unwillingly, when buoyant or not, buy on credit or pay cash for **credits, data bundles** and **subscriptions** to avoid disconnection weekly, monthly or periodically as prepaid and postpaid customers to the providers. Some professionals who are working class and salary earners budget for **the three** from the monthly pay before they even buy foodstuff and wears. It is a topmost priority to use apps to deduct all revenues such as taxes at the sources.

Again, on the part of the communications and information sectors in the ministries and their regulatory agencies, if all these payments have proper documentations and dependable statistics from the office of bureau of statistics, the **deductions of the VATs at the source** for the nation to generate huge revenues that are buoyant enough to fund all laudable projects, then such is free from stringent conditions of borrowing from creditors!

Conclusively, the nation, Nigeria, is blessed from the soaring mobile market consumers to generate **several hundreds of billions if not trillions per month** from the proceeds of the VATs and other taxes and levies deductible from the points of transactions (POTs). This is what called for software that would credit the nation's account from each recharge of the communications devices.

PART FIVE
BRAINS STORMING EXERCISES AND TESTS

a) Identify at least five economic problems in the named-market and suggest practicable solutions for the economic teams of the nation
b) A nation is in a political impasse. List some of the probable causes of political logjam in a nation and proffer some solutions. How best can you pass the message recommended as solutions to the problems?
c) You are a witness to fatal accident. List the steps you would rightly take to reach out to the ministry before others in order to enjoy the cash rewards for the reports.
d) Develop software that would contain all the information of credit sales per day.
e) Create a portal to synergize the sales and marketing department of a mobile network operator.

PUBLICATION REFERENCES

Emeka Aginam (2015) <u>Nigerian Computers Society (NCS) presents 10-point agenda to Buhari</u> Vanguard Dec; 9 page 25-32

Everest Amaefule (2015) <u>Nigeria slides to 134th in ICT devt index</u> The Punch, Dec; 1 page 36

Ozioma Ubabukoh (2015) <u>NCC targets 25% ICT contribution to GDP</u> The Punch, Dec; 1, page 38

Ditto (2015) <u>Nigeria loses 2,175 websites, N159 billion to cybercriminals</u> The Punch Dec; 3 page 34

ABOUT THE BOOK

This book gives concise **insight** into **simple ways** the nation can generate over one trillion naira per month from the effectiveness and efficiency of the staff members of the ministry and regulatory agencies under it particularly the use of apps or electronic payment of taxes, VATS and other tariffs at the source from the communications and information sectors in collaboration with other ministries, departments and agencies of government.

In the researched-based book are lucid ways and arsenals for the ministry with simple reforms that cost the ministry **zero naira** except the redeployments and re-energizing the departments on the new tasks at hand in internet-based environment.

The book also contains simple guides to ensure reforms of the MDAs, the telecoms sector and the staff members to nip the institutional ills against wealth and employment creation from the intellectual researches for the growth and development of all the strata of the nation.

Overall, the billions being fairly generated by the illustrations in the book would go a long way to turn the communications ministry into a *cash cow* for increase in the GNI and improvement on GDP and take the nation away from heavy dependence from the proceeds from oil revenues and borrowing to fund budgets.

ABOUT THE AUTHOR

He is a creative and prolific writer who has authored two international books on employment creation namely "Jobs with zero-capital Vol. One" and "Creating new jobs from the existing jobs'. Both books can be found in **twelve world libraries** including the **British Library** whose audience level is 80% as at the fourth quarter of 2015 (**worldcat.org**). His follow-up books like "Winning huge sales and increasing clients' base" and "Piracy, the causes, the trends and the practicable solutions" guide those who start new jobs and the existing businesses to be successful in the business environment.

As a **think-tank**, his sole thinking which kick starts researches is to proffer solutions to issues and this prompted his research into producing this work to transform the nation, **Nigeria,** and others on the same platform from the **third world nation** to the **first world** within a short time of **three years**!

RECOMMENDED AND REFERENTIAL BOOKS FROM THE SAME AUTHOR

a) Path from fourth world to the first world
b) If I aspire to lead.....
c) Over 200 reasons why abundantly endowed nations are poor
d) Restructuring of education, economy, politics, judiciary and resource control
e) Economic recession, the causes, the spiral effects and the practicable solutions
f) Getting wealthy your own way

www.ingramcontent.com/pod-product-compliance
Lightning Source LLC
Chambersburg PA
CBHW020433220526
45464CB00002B/681